UNSILENCING THE PAST

UNSILENCING THE PAST

Track Two Diplomacy and
Turkish-Armenian Reconciliation

David L. Phillips

Berghahn Books
New York • Oxford

First published in 2005 by

Berghahn Books
www.berghahnbooks.com

©2005 David L. Phillips

Library of Congress Cataloging-in-Publication Data
Phillips, David L.
   Unsilencing the past : track two diplomacy and Turkish-Armenian rec-
onciliation / David L. Phillips.
     p. cm.
   ISBN 1-84545-007-8
   1. Armenian question. 2. Reconciliation. 3. Conflict management—
Turkey.
   4. Turkey—Ethnic relations. I. Title.
   DS195.P35 2004
   327.1'7'09475609561—dc22

                                             2004056032

British Library Cataloguing in Publication Data
A catalogue record for this book is available from the British Library

Printed in the United States on acid-free paper

ISBN 1-84545-007-8 hardback

DEDICATION

To my mother and father—whose lifelong commitment to social justice is a constant inspiration.

And to the victims of atrocities—may the memory of their suffering prevent future generations from violence and affliction.

CONTENTS

ACKNOWLEDGMENTS

This book is about the Turkish-Armenian Reconciliation Commission (TARC) and other Turks and Armenians who participated in Track Two activities. Their courageous efforts deserve special commendation.

The initiative was made possible by my mentors in the U.S. Government. I am grateful for the encouragement and support of Richard C. Holbrooke, Marc Grossman, Tom Miller and Helena Kane Finn.

I am also grateful to my collaborators at American University's Center for Global Peace: Abdul Aziz Said, Betty Sitka, Rachel Pentlarge and Stephen Ladek.

PREFACE

by Elie Wiesel

David Phillips's informative and stimulating ideas on how to resolve conflicts by using Track Two diplomacy find their expression in this volume. Filled with personal recollections as well as historical references, it deals with contemporary issues between Turks and Armenians. I hope it will be read by students of international relations everywhere.

Is his approach original? Has it been fruitful? Whatever the answer, it had to be tried.

Clearly, the endeavor encountered various obstacles: ancestral hate is not easily erased. Memory of past defeats is not necessarily a shield against warfare. Only rarely, in moments of grace, does one side accept the other.

David evokes my modest participation in the endeavor. Rather than compose a lengthy commentary on his own involvement, I offer the reader the text of what I said at David's Track Two meeting:

* * *

Is there an endeavor more urgent and more challenging than bringing people together and moving them toward reconciliation? If only we could celebrate peace as our various ancestors celebrated war; if only we could glorify peace as those before us, thirsting for adventure and conquest, glorified war; if only our sages and scholars, poets and philosophers, could together resolve to infuse peace with the same energy and inspiration that they or others have put into warfare.

Why is war such an easy option? Why does peace remain such an elusive goal? We know statesmen skilled at waging war, but where are those dedicated enough to humanity to find a way to avoid war?

Every nation has its prestigious military academies. Why are there no academies (or so few of them) that teach not only the virtues of peace but also the art of attaining it? Why are we so thankful yet surprised whenever war recedes and yields to peace?

Oh, I know: people will blame human nature. They will tell us that since the origins of history, violence and bloodshed dominated society. Lest we forget, the story of Cain and Abel must forever serve as a warning. They were brothers and yet one became the murderer and/or victim of the other. Is that the lesson we derive from that biblical story? That brothers can become enemies and kill one another? No. The lesson is that whoever kills, kills his brother. And this so many warriors prefer to forget.

Why?

War puts an end to questions. Military and political orders replace civilized language. Thinking is dangerous, doubting, forbidden. Everything is oversimplified. If only the soldier on the front line could imagine the humanity of the human being he is about to maim or kill—would he still pull the trigger or drop the bomb? In time of war, imagination is also a victim. In time of conflict, whoever is not our brother is our enemy—rather than the reverse. Why can't we all agree once and for all that, on a purely human level, all wars are fratricidal? That is why warfare is ultimately to be seen not only as cruel but also as grotesque and ugly. And true soldiers are the first to acknowledge it. They know there can be no beauty, no poetry, no art, no humanity, no redemptive impulse—except one of revulsion and protest—on a battlefield covered with mutilated and muted corpses.

Who or what is responsible for war among nations and communities? Strategic considerations, nationalism, and economic interests were often blamed, and rightly so. Religion, too, has played a role in their outbreak, as has ethnic affiliation. The factors were varied, the consequences remained the same: they represented an intolerable desecration of human life and an unbearable profanation of human values.

Thus, the real answer to war is to avoid it, to prevent it, to replace it with something—or anything—else. But once war has been waged, the memory of its brutality must lead to reconciliation. For just as deadly conflict is a scourge, reconciliation is a remedy. A challenge to what causes suffering, weakness, and death, it is a noble man's most noble way of transcending the vulnerability of his or her condition.

Oh yes, there is greatness, more precisely: moral greatness in the sight of enemies meeting, shaking hands, engaging in dialogue leading to reconciliation. Their gesture turns into a powerful defiance of selfishness and evil.

All of you have maintained alive your respective traditions of serving your peoples with honor—won't you become their benefactors by seeking an end to the reign of hatred and inevitable violence that cost so many lives?

We all know that there are reasons, maybe even valid reasons not to forget what the other side has done to your families and friends. Memory could easily become a lethal weapon in the name of hatred rather than a shield against lethal instincts, inviting comradeship and brotherhood. Do not let it happen. Use memory and its lessons as a bridge reconciling friend and foe, East and West, Islam and Christianity.

Better yet: it was not easy for the Jewish people in Israel to enter into a blessed period of reconciliation with Germany. Think about it: if Jews and Germans can cooperate within the framework of humanizing History, others can too. It does not imply forgetting the past. That would be an act of betrayal. The past can not be erased for the sake of the future. Quite the contrary: it is because we remember the past that together we feel responsible for what tomorrow may bring to all our children.

Granted, the past has its reasons—but so does the future. I say that because I belong to a generation that felt betrayed by man and abandoned by God; it had all the reasons in the world not to trust society—and yet we remain part of it. It could have given up on "the other"—and yet we aspire to make him or her into allies. It could have treated culture and education with disdain—and yet we continue to be nourished by them. It could have discarded reason, compassion, and kindness as ways of life—and yet we are determined to proclaim them as noble goals without which the future would look bleak and History senseless, absurd, and ultimately unworthy of being remembered. Let us learn from each other's suffering and we shall realize that we are all children of the same Father. We are all equally entitled to benefit from His creation just as we are equally responsible for its welfare. No people is superior or inferior to another. No nation is worthier than another. No religion is holier than another. Racism is both stupid and sinful, and ethnic discrimination outrageous. Religious fanaticism leads to hatred, not to salvation, just as political extremism begets hostility, not security. When a group—for ethnic, religious, or ideological reasons—claims its superiority over others, it only shows its will to dominate others.

We know this from history. There has never been a generation without some nations being coveted and conquered by others, some freedoms curtailed and abolished by others, people killed by others, believers persecuted and humbled by other believers.

Is it that the human condition must forever confront its own destruction from within and without? Will society never learn that to accept violence as an option will help Death increase its power and stretch its boundaries to the farthest horizons? Will we ever realize that wars are useless, for victories never last long?

As the century draws to its end, one cannot but wonder: what will its legacy be? What will it leave to the next one? Only its stunning technological triumphs, which overshadowed its moral shortcomings?

There is much anguish around us, perhaps even in us. Too many projects have gone wrong. Idealism has been corrupted, principles abused. The quest for truth was addressed in falsehood, the search for peace in bloodshed. Is there a place on the planet that is not threatened? Is there an ideal that has not aroused suspicion? I am worried. Many of us are. Humankind is in a train running towards the abyss. Unless we pull the alarm, it may be too late.

Isn't it time to stop and show the world that together we embody not only man's dignity but also his and her hope?

* * *

This is why David Phillips's book is so important; it responds to a need. To read it is to commit oneself to peace, which is the noblest of all goals. To attain it one must confront both sides of a conflict in Track Two diplomatic efforts and engage each of them in dialogue about the other. Our role would begin as intermediary and then as mediator but would soon be transcended into that of intercessor who makes impossible dreams possible.

INTRODUCTION

The world is full of intractable conflicts that confound traditional diplomacy. Practitioners of conflict resolution may derive lessons from the endeavor described on these pages. Rather than writing an academic treatise, I have tried to humanize the work of Turks and Armenians by recounting their struggle to confront a tormented past and explore future cooperation. Their experience is instructive to other conflicts mired in historic enmity.

I was not trained in Track Two diplomacy, nor am I a scholar of Ottoman history or Turkish studies. My work on Turkish-Armenian issues emerged from a decade trying to foster dialogue between Turks and Kurds. I subsequently got involved with Cypriots and with Greeks and Turks. These initiatives are called "Track Two." Track Two activities create a context for civil society to develop mutual understanding with the goal of transferring their insights to decision-makers and shaping public opinion.

* * *

Marc Grossman, U.S. Undersecretary of State for Political Affairs, warned me that Track Two diplomacy involving Turks and Armenians would be my most difficult task yet. Turks and Armenians have a deep distrust toward each other. They are divided by different perceptions of history and separated by a border closed to travel and trade. Central to their disagreement is the huge gap in national perceptions over events that occurred during the waning years of the Ottoman Empire.

Armenians describe bloody pogroms in the late nineteenth century resulting in the death of an estimated quarter million Armenians. On April 24, 1915, eight hundred Armenian community leaders were rounded up and deported. More than a million Armenians perished between 1915 and 1923.[1] A Turkish court subsequently convicted the "Young Turks" of planning and implementing the extermination of the Armenian people.

Turkey rejects use of the term "genocide" and objects to the campaign of the Armenian Diaspora to gain international recognition. Some Turks dispute the facts and underscore the war context in which events occurred. They claim that the Armenians betrayed the Ottoman Empire by waging a decades-long rebellion and collaborating with the Russian army to achieve independence. With the communist revolution, Tsarist forces withdrew protection for Armenians who were deemed a security risk and deported. Turkey acknowledges that several hundred thousand Armenians were killed; Kurdish bandits are blamed. Turkey also insists that the Armenians killed at least an equal number of Turks during their insurgency.

Armenians are not the only ones who suffered. Many Turks have a family lore about loss, injustice, and humiliation. Turks were also driven from their homes in the Balkans, the Caucasus, and the Black Sea region.

Close historical and cultural ties bind Anatolian Turks to their brethren in Central Asia and the Caspian region. Turkey reacted when, in 1988, hostilities broke out in Nagorno-Karabakh, an ethnic Armenian enclave in Azerbaijan. Armenian forces occupied a large chunk of Azeri territory. As a result of the conflict, more than twenty thousand people died and a million were displaced. Turkey imposed a blockade severing Armenia's overland ties to the West. Though Ankara recognizes the state of Armenia, it refuses to establish formal diplomatic relations until Azerbaijan's "occupied territories" are returned.

Despite their physical proximity, Turks and Armenians have had remarkably little contact over the past eighty-five years. Until recently, "Armenian issues" were totally taboo in Turkey. On the other hand, every Armenian recalls the death of family members expelled from ancestral lands around Mount Ararat and large swaths of territory in what is now eastern Turkey.

* * *

Track Two is an unofficial exercise in problem solving. It engages private citizens in exploring the conditions that give rise to conflict and developing joint strategies for addressing shared problems. The goal is to foster collaboration so that conflict comes to be seen as a shared problem requiring the cooperation of both sides. Though the virtue of Track Two lies in its independence from official positions, Track Two can enhance diplomacy when developed in close coordination with diplomatic efforts.

The *Track Two Program on Turkey and the Caucasus* was initiated during the Clinton administration and formally established in 2001. The program's centerpiece was the Turkish-Armenian Reconciliation Commission (TARC) made up of prominent Turks and Armenians, including former officials and civil society leaders. When it was announced, TARC was heralded as a historic step addressing historical issues and potentially fostering better relations between Turkey and Armenia. TARC also helped break the ice by encouraging other civil society contacts engaged in Track Two. As TARC evolved into a broader "consultative group" involving civil society in both countries, it fostered an environment encouraging Armenians and Turks to meet, develop personal bonds, and find new ways to deal with difficult problems. They have been able to look over the horizon and envision the benefits of cooperation.

For example, Armenian and Turkish folk and classical musicians are performing together. Journalists exchange columns. Women's groups collaborate and a women's magazine has been copublished. A documentary on Turkish-Armenian cultural events is to be aired in both countries. Local chambers of commerce explore commercial opportunities. Innovative web-based technologies are used in the "Virtual Agricultural Wholesale Market" and a Task Force on Regional Economic Cooperation promotes business. Restoration experts are developing plans to rebuild Akhtamar, one of the most sacred and ancient Armenian Churches in Turkey. Academic exchanges take place and sociologists work together to research mutual perceptions. Parliamentarians, local government officials, and mayors in border towns have been trained in mediation and cross-cultural communication.

Meetings typically involve Armenians and Turks. Some also include Azeris. It is difficult, however, to bring Azeris and Armenians together. While Armenians are keen to engage, most Azeris insist that relations are impossible as long as Armenians control Azerbaijan's territory.

* * *

Conflicts cast a long shadow. Despite various efforts to promote dialogue, Armenian militants condemn contact with Turks until Turkey returns territory and pays reparations. In turn, Turkish hard-liners insist that Armenians agree there was no genocide at all. Armenians cannot go forward absent a reckoning with the past; Turks prefer to forget the past and focus on the future; Azerbaijan demands the return of territory as a precondition for dialogue.

To break the logjam, TARC requested the International Center for Transitional Justice to "facilitate the provision of an independent legal analysis on the applicability of the United Nations Genocide Convention on the Prevention and Punishment of the Crime of Genocide to events which occurred during the early twentieth century."[2] Though the analysis was risky in addressing the most divisive issue between Turks and

Armenians, it offered both sides just enough to feel that their interests were affirmed. The full impact of the analysis will take several years.

Turks welcomed the core finding. International law generally prohibits the retroactive application of treaties. No legal, financial, or territorial claim arising out of the events could successfully be made under the Convention. Armenians also found elements to their liking. The analysis concluded that "At least some of the perpetrators knew that the consequence of their actions would be the destruction of, in whole or in part, the Armenians of eastern Anatolia, as such, or acted purposefully towards this goal and, therefore, possessed the requisite genocidal intent. The term genocide can be applied to events that occurred prior to the entry into force of the Convention (9 December 1948)."[3]

It was unprecedented for a group of Turks and Armenians to request a legal analysis on such a contentious issue. The endeavor could only have occurred via Track Two. Governments would never be so bold. In addition to addressing historical issues, TARC took the lead urging Turkey and Armenia to open the border as part of a process culminating in the normalization of diplomatic relations.

* * *

The *Track Two Program on Turkey and the Caucasus* is by no means the first time Track Two has been used in global problem solving. There are many examples involving, for example, Protestants and Catholics in Northern Ireland, Tamils and Sinhalese in Sri Lanka, Indians and Pakistanis, and Israelis and Palestinians. What makes this program unique is its systematic approach, as well as its concentrated and continuous activity. The effort would not have been possible without assistance from the U.S. State Department. Austrian, Swedish, Swiss, and British institutions also supported the endeavor.

The United States and the international community have several stakes in promoting better relations between Turkey and Armenia. Not only are both countries valued allies and important partners in the war against terrorism, but also regional peace, stability, and economic prosperity are problematic without resolution of differences between the neighboring countries. Globalization and regional integration make national boundaries less important and render obstacles to regional cooperation increasingly obsolete. To strengthen their ties with the community of democracies, Armenians and Turks are seizing opportunities to advance their shared interests and common objectives.

By taking the first steps, Turks and Armenians have helped make the climate more conducive for official contact. In January 2002, Ankara reinstated a process for Armenian passport holders to receive visas when flying to Turkey. The foreign ministers of Armenia and Turkey and their deputies have been meeting regularly to explore economic cooperation and discuss transportation arrangements. Turkish and Armenian officials accepted TARC's final report as the basis for future talks on Turkish-Armenian relations. Today, Track Two activities are in full swing. Detractors claimed Track Two was a poor substitute for official diplomacy. They were wrong. The Track Two program spurred political discourse at the official level. It also catalyzed Turkish and Armenian civil society to seek contact and cooperation.

The Turkish-Armenian conflict is one of the world's most intractable problems entailing both historical and contemporary issues. It involves neighboring states, several other countries, as well as Diaspora interests. The problem is further complicated by Cold War and antiterrorism politics. The *Track Two Program for Turkey and the Caucasus* is not a textbook for other Track Two endeavors, but its successes and failures are instructive.

Reflecting on the effort to promote reconciliation between Turks and Armenians, Elie Wiesel, the 1986 Nobel Peace Prize recipient, said, "I see this event as a miracle. If Turks and Armenians can meet and talk, that means others can do it too."[4] Unsilencing the past is the key to creating opportunities in the future. This book tells the story of Turks and Armenians who struggled to advance the goal of reconciliation.

Notes

1. Figures are contested.
2. TARC statement issued on November 21, 2001.
3. International Center for Transitional Justice, February 2003.
4. Douglas Frantz, *New York Times,* July 9, 2001.

1

Lessons from
the Eastern Mediterranean

My first visit to Turkey was soon after the Gulf War. I crossed the border between Turkey and Iraq at what was once an obscure truck stop named Habur. When the UN imposed sanctions on Iraq after the Gulf War, Habur became a major transit point for smuggled Iraqi oil. The road was covered by a thick oil slick for miles on either side of the border.

The route to the Kurdish region of northern Iraq goes through Diyarbakir, the largest city in southeastern Turkey. On my way back from Salahuddin, I was dropped on the Iraqi side of the border and walked across to find a Turkish taxi. Though the drive should have only been a couple of hours, it took all day. I was stopped repeatedly at checkpoints by Turkish police who detained and interrogated me. They were concerned that I was in the area to contact the Kurdistan Workers' Party (PKK), a pro-independence group of Turkish Kurds identified as a terrorist organization by the United States.

My initial experience with Track Two involved Turks and Kurds. Their first structured dialogue occurred at a chateau outside of Paris. After warily testing the waters, a Kurdish participant told his personal story. He described numerous arrests and his torture in detention. On one occasion, his jailers forced him to eat his feces and drink his own urine. Tragedy also touched his family. His son died from an "accident" while in custody. One of the meeting participants was a retired admiral in the Turkish navy who was horrified to hear about atrocities committed by the state in his name. Repentantly, he offered an apology on behalf of the Turkish people. Their exchange was a defining moment in the process. Storytelling is an important component of Track Two.

Over the next six months, the Turks and Kurds met again at a villa on Lake Lugano in Switzerland and finally at an old monastery in Belgium. Participants adopted a charter called "Walking Together in History," which described their shared hopes as citizens of Turkey. They also decided to continue their cooperation by setting up an Ankara-based democracy organization to disseminate their findings to the broader public. Marc Grossman, who was serving as the U.S. ambassador to Turkey at the time, lauded our success institutionalizing cooperation between Turks and Kurds.

* * *

During the 1990s, I was also involved in the Balkans and had the privilege of working with Ambassador Richard C. Holbrooke, who negotiated the Dayton Peace Agreement ending Bosnia's bloody war in November 1995. Holbrooke's qualities of vision and tenacity, which served him so well in the Balkans, were also useful in his role as special envoy for Cyprus to which he was appointed by President Clinton in 1998. Despite the logic of Holbrooke's envisioned solution for Cyprus—a bizonal, bicommunal federation with power distributed between the entities— brokering a deal would be daunting even for someone with his uncanny instincts and negotiating skills.

The modern political history of Cyprus is littered with international mediators. All had failed to finalize an arrangement between Glafco Clerides, president of the Republic of Cyprus, and Rauf Denktash, the Turkish Cypriot leader. To build momentum for formal talks, Holbrooke plotted a Track Two initiative involving Greek and Turkish Cypriot business leaders. I was hired as a senior advisor to the State Department in January 1999.

On my first trip to Cyprus in September 1998, I was studying the briefing book provided by the American embassy in Nicosia. It contained mostly trivia—history, hotels, and contact numbers. I was struck, however, by one piece of advice. When asking for coffee, say "medium." Coffee preference could indicate political bias. Asking for Turkish coffee in Greek Nicosia was strictly taboo.

Words matter to Cypriots. For example, the events of July 1974 are characterized as an "invasion" by Greek Cypriots and as an "intervention" by Turkish Cypriots. Referring to Rauf Denktash, the Turkish Cypriot leader, as "President Denktash" or "Mr. Denktash" reveals one's political perspective. The so-called Turkish Republic of Northern Cyprus (TRNC) is recognized only by the authorities in Ankara.

Cyprus is the last divided country in Europe. A Berlin-like wall runs across the island separating north from south. In 1963, the Greek military junta engineered a coup against Cypriot president Makarios. When coup leaders abolished the constitution, the stage was set for the annexation of Cyprus to Greece—"Enosis."

Claiming that the 1960 Treaty of Guarantee provided a legal basis for intervening, Turkey's prime minister, Bulent Ecevit, launched a military action during the summer of 1974. Properties were possessed, families were divided, and many civilians disappeared during the conflict. When Turkey took steps to expand territory under its control, the U.S. Congress responded by imposing an arms embargo in 1980. Three years later, the UN Security Council formally rejected claims of legitimacy by the TRNC. The division of Cyprus left Turks with 38 percent of the island, including the best beaches and northern resort areas. Greek Cypriots retain the balance of territory, which contains the island's agro-industrial and commercial centers.

When I got involved, relations between Greece and Turkey were at a low point. In January 1996, competing groups raised Greek and Turkish national flags on the island known as Imia (in Greek) and Kardak (in Turkish). The incident almost triggered a war between the NATO allies and crystallized the competing claims of Greece and Turkey over territorial waters. As permitted by the International Convention on the Law of the Sea, Athens extended its continental shelf from six to twelve miles. Since the move effectively choked off Turkey's access to the Greater Aegean, Ankara viewed the extension as a *causus belli*.

Plans by Cyprus to buy Russian Krug missiles risked changing the balance of power in the Eastern Aegean. Tensions heightened even further when, a few days prior to my arrival in Cyprus, the Greek defense minister's plane was accosted by Turkish F-16s. Routine tit-for-tat confrontations kept Greece and Turkey on the edge of war.

After several days of discussions with Greek Cypriots, I crossed the green line in the U.S. ambassador's car. No one was allowed to pass the fortified boundary, but the gate opened wide for us at the Ledra Palace crossing. During my meetings with Turkish Cypriots in the city and at "Embassy North," I was struck by the enormous gap between North and South Cyprus. The Greek side of Nicosia was bustling and prosperous with streets that shimmered like the Champs-Elysées. The other side looked liked Istanbul's worst slums. In exchange for their quasi-independence, Turkish Cypriots suffer deprivation and impoverishment from an international embargo to which every country adheres except Turkey.

* * *

Holbrooke invited a dozen Greek Cypriots, a dozen Turkish Cypriots, and a dozen Greeks and Turks to a conference entitled "In Economic Cooperation Lies Mutual Benefit." The Norwegian government covered the costs of the meeting, which was held in Brussels in November 1997. I asked Jan Egeland, famous for his role in the Oslo Accords, to cochair the meeting with Holbrooke.

At the opening ceremonies, Holbrooke explained, "Track Two is separate from substantive negotiations. The whole point is to get people together who are not in governments, to talk with each other about things they can do on a people to people basis. This process does not itself resolve core issues—strategic, political and historical—that divide peoples. But it does create bridges of understanding which break down the barriers."[1]

A cast of luminaries was in attendance. Dick Spring, the former foreign minister of Ireland, described Ireland's experience and highlighted the benefits from interethnic cooperation for a small island economy. Sir David Hannay, the U.K.'s Cyprus negotiator, described three categories of cooperation: activities that the business communities can undertake on their own; steps the business communities could take with government cooperation; and problems only governments can address. The strategy for resolving Cyprus was based on the conviction that Turkey, whose prospects for joining the European Union (EU) would improve after a Cyprus solution, could move Rauf Denktash to compromise. Echoing this message, EU Commissioner Hans van den Broek presented his thoughts on Turkey's relations with the European Union.

During my earlier fact-finding trip to Cyprus, I attended a briefing at the UN headquarters and saw an old telephone switchboard in one of the back offices. The switchboard operator was manually inserting telephone wires to connect callers. When queried, she described that the switchboard used an old telephone cable to connect "emergency calls" between north and south. I reasoned that, if a few phone calls could be made, upgrading the system could enable many more.

Holbrooke immediately seized on the benefits of getting people talking. Engineers found that expanding the existing cable and computerizing the system could service up to one million calls each year. Arrangements were made and the resumption of phone service was announced at the Brussels conference. When the system was inaugurated on May 5, 1998, it was flooded with calls. Apparently, Cypriots were desperate to speak with each other after so many years. On a small island where intercommunal contact was all but impossible, being able to make a phone call was significant.

* * *

According to Holbrooke, "Discussions were intense, engaged and at times even electrifying. There was a real quality in the room, an exciting quality." Conference participants agreed to institutionalize their work, affirming "the importance of contact and cooperation between the two communities. Most importantly, this includes steps to relax and eventually lift all restrictions on the free movement of people, goods and services and increase contact regarding specific projects for the benefit of all the people of Cyprus."[2]

They planned to establish a headquarters at the Ledra Palace. They also agreed on special projects including an island-wide telephone directory and a cross-island courier service. Dozens of other bicommunal activities were proposed. The Track Two endeavor created a sense of possibility. Capitalizing on the public outcry for progress, Holbrooke brought Clerides and Denktash together for a famous caviar feast and their first face-to-face meeting in years.

Hope was short-lived. Momentum arising from the Brussels conference came to an abrupt halt after the EU Luxembourg summit in December 1997. Not only was Turkey excluded from both the first and second tiers of prospective members, it was not even referred to as a candidate. Luxembourg's Prime Minister Jean-Claude Juncker added salt to the wound by proclaiming, "A country in which torture is still a common practice cannot have a seat at the table of the European Union."[3]

Turks were deeply insulted. Denktash banned all bicommunal contacts and even tried to prohibit off-island meetings between civil society groups. Prodded by Denktash and in protest of the continuing economic embargo, Turkish Cypriots questioned the viability of discussions on economic cooperation. The situation worsened when the Republic of Cyprus failed to include representatives of the TRNC in the official Cypriot delegation negotiating EU accession.

Turkish Cypriots initially refused to attend when we invited them to a follow-up meeting in Oslo. Defying pressure from Denktash, one person finally broke ranks and then others followed. Sarik Tara, the owner of a big Turkish construction company, helped by rounding up members of the delegation and flying them in his private plane to Oslo.

Elie Wiesel, the Nobel Peace Prize recipient and Holocaust survivor, opened the Oslo conference. He reminded Cypriots that they were not the only people to suffer. He urged them to set aside the narcissism of small differences and move forward on the path of reconciliation. Participants were inspired and reaffirmed their willingness to work together.

Many projects were discussed. Participants agreed to restore the historical monuments of Apostolos Andreas, an Eastern Orthodox monastery on the Turkish side, and Hala Sultan, a Turkish monument in the south. Other joint activities were identified in the fields of telecommunications, environmental protection, culture, and sport. One especially creative initiative involved the Careta sea turtle, an endangered species that circumnavigates the island during its breeding cycle. Study tours for marine biologists were proposed. If turtles can travel across the island, tourists could too.

At the next meeting in Istanbul, discussions focused on collaborative activities to address the acute water shortage in Cyprus. Tara, who saved the day in Oslo, announced that his construction and engineering firm would investigate building a "water peace pipeline" from Turkey's Manavgat River in Antalya to northern Cyprus.[4] In early 1999, the Republic of Cyprus sent staff from the Department of Water Resources to meet with water engineers from the north at the U.S. Geological Service. Clerides was concerned that the workshop would be manipulated to imply official recognition of the TRNC, and almost cancelled the meeting at the last moment. When participants finally arrived, I was struck by the positive feeling between them. Guided by international specialists at a neutral venue, technical experts from north and south overcame political, cultural, and language barriers to conduct substantive discussions on an island-wide water plan. I helped arrange a grant of $1 million to support the Water Resources Database Development Project. Ultimately more than fifty bicommunal projects were planned. To galvanize follow-through and local leadership, a full-time Norwegian representative was assigned to work on bicommunal projects in Cyprus.

* * *

By this point, it was clear that a Cyprus settlement would require impetus from Greece and Turkey. EU membership was the magnet linking Greek and Turkish interests in a common future and, in the process, enabling cooperation on Cyprus. Mediators tried to convince Greece that it should lift its objection to Turkey's EU candidacy. They argued that when Turkey met EU criteria, it would become a better neighbor, a stronger economic partner, and a significantly reduced threat.

I shifted my focus to Greek-Turkish relations, reaching out to Greeks and Turks with whom I had forged relationships during our Track Two meetings on Cyprus. We made plans to revitalize the Greek-Turkish Business Council, establish a Greek-Turkish media group, and arrange joint projects between Greek and Turkish scholars, particularly historians. Sabanci University in Istanbul established joint working groups on commerce, education, culture, and tourism, which would ultimately set the stage for bilateral agreements between Greece and Turkey.

On February 15, 1999, I arrived in Athens for another round of meetings with Greek business leaders. Tom Miller, who would later become America's ambassador to Greece, had arranged an all-star lineup of appointments with some of the country's leading industrialists and shipping magnates. Traffic was snarled coming in from the airport. My driver explained that Kurds were demonstrating and that several had lit themselves on fire. They were protesting the arrest of Abdullah Ocalan, chief of the PKK.

Ocalan was at the top of Turkey's "most wanted" list. Following a world-wide manhunt, he was apprehended and whisked to Imrali Prison on an isolated island near the Dardanelles. On the run for more than a month after being expelled from Syria, Ocalan's movements were tracked from the Netherlands to Russia and a villa in Rome. He finally ended up at the Greek embassy in Nairobi. U.S. and Israeli intelligence were monitoring his movements and they alerted Turkish authorities. Ilter Turkmen, who served as Turkey's foreign minister from 1980 to 1983, told me, "The U.S. delivered Ocalan to us like they delivered a pizza—and then let us take credit for it."[5]

Ocalan's arrest sparked a nationwide celebration in Turkey. Though Kurds in Turkey suffered terrible abuses, the PKK was never effective in advancing the legitimate aspirations of Turkish Kurds for greater political and cultural rights. Thousands of Kurdish villages were razed for harboring the PKK. Ocalan's fighters targeted the armed forces, the police, and village guards, as well as Kurdish civil servants who cooperated with Turkish authorities. Kurdish civilians were tragically caught in the middle of an armed conflict between the Turkish army and the PKK.

Turks were incensed when they learned that Greece was harboring Ocalan. Their anger was exacerbated by reports that Greeks provided financial and military assistance to the PKK. Turkey accused Greece of being a state sponsor of terrorism; Greek authorities responded with charges that Turkey's thinly disguised dictatorship had brought the Kurdish problem on itself. The war of words reversed a positive trend in Greek-Turkish relations. Greece and Turkey had agreed to establish joint subregional commands under NATO. They also agreed to jointly spearhead a rapid deployment task force for peacekeeping operations in the Balkans. However, the Ocalan fiasco sent Greek-Turkish relations into a tailspin. Official contact was broken off.

Civil society efforts also suffered; Rahmi Koc resigned as cochair of the Greek-Turkish Business Council, but Tara heroically kept the dialogue going. Alexis Papahelas and Mehmet Ali Birand, who worked with me to organize teams of Greek and Turkish journalists, continued to meet. So did academics coordinated by Sabanci University in Istanbul and Panteion University in Athens. Through their collaborative work, these civil society networks acted as a safety net. They maintained dialogue when officials in both countries would not. Financial support from the American embassies in Athens and Ankara was invaluable. So was the optimism of Dr. Helena Kane Finn, Counselor for Public Affairs at the U.S. Embassy in Ankara. Helena would emerge as Track Two's great champion, and she later played a pivotal role in supporting the *Track Two Program on Turkey and the Caucasus*.

NATO's war with Yugoslavia slowed the negative spiral in Greek-Turkish relations with Greece and Turkey finding common cause in opposing military action in Kosovo. In solidarity with their Christian Orthodox brothers, Greeks sympathized with Serbs and opposed the war. Fearing that support for ethnic Albanian separatists might set a precedent vis-à-vis Kurds in Turkey, Ankara was just as reluctant to endorse military action. Through NATO, the Kosovo conflict required Greek and Turkish militaries to cooperate on a daily basis delivering supplies, reinforcements, and coordinating humanitarian assistance to almost a million Kosovar refugees on the Macedonian border and in Albania. Greece's foreign minister, George Papandreou, met his Turkish counterpart, Ismail Cem, at the North Atlantic Council meeting on April 24, 1999. A few weeks later, they met again under the auspices of the "Friends of the UN Secretary-General on Kosovo."

Building on their personal chemistry, Cem sent Papandreou a letter on May 24 proposing "joint efforts combating terrorism." On June 30, both foreign ministers assigned political directors to begin discussions. Instead of focusing on territorial waters and Cyprus, they agreed to work together on regional problems in the Balkans, the Caucasus, and the Middle East. By avoiding the most difficult issues, expectations were intentionally kept low.

When a devastating earthquake struck Turkey on August 17, killing more than 20,000 people, Greek aid organizations were among the first to respond. When a second, less powerful earthquake hit Greece, the mutual outpouring of sympathy spurred support for government policies to improve the bilateral relationship.[6] Papandreou applauded "human solidarity in the face of national tragedy. People have dared to think what we politicians believed was impossible. They have gone beyond our diplomatic maneuvers. In a glorious moment, they have taken diplomacy into their own hands."[7]

By the end of 1999, Greece lifted its long-standing objections to Turkey's EU candidacy. Bilateral agreements were reached in the areas of trade; tariffs; anticrime, antiterrorism, illegal immigration; environmental protection; tourism; and cultural and educational exchanges. Multilateral cooperation was advanced through the Black Sea Economic Cooperation Council and via the Southeastern Europe Cooperation Initiative.

Opportunities for Greek-Turkish rapprochement had ripened and political leaders from both countries had the courage to take meaningful steps. Col. Stephen R. Norton, U.S. Army, Ret., notes, "Greeks and Turks [became] accustomed to the notion that they can coexist in a non-zero-sum world. A more cordial relationship that marginalizes nationalism and extremism and allows for working progress that benefits both countries is of irrefutable interest to both Greece and Turkey. The future of

Greek-Turkish relations lies in the recognition that interdependence and globalization are overtaking the world. National isolation, especially on the part of powerful, prosperous and neighboring allies, is a dead end."[8]

Despite progress, core areas of disagreement still remain. The Aegean dispute continues to impede rapprochement. Greece's extension of the continental shelf and territorial waters is deeply resented by Ankara. In between scheduled military exercises, there are still occasional confrontations between Greek and Turkish forces at sea and in airspace over the Eastern Mediterranean.[9]

Cyprus also remains a sore spot. In 2002, UN Secretary-General Kofi Annan personally intervened to advance a settlement before the European Union invited Cyprus to start accession talks. The Annan proposal met most of the criteria that Turkey had insisted upon over the years, including a highly decentralized federation, the right to veto decisions, and security guarantees enforced by thousands of Turkish troops. Initially, Turkey refused to pressure Denktash. When he rejected the UN proposal, the EU went ahead and offered membership to Cyprus at the Copenhagen summit in December 2002. Despite the UN's efforts, the Annan Plan ultimately failed when Greek Cypriots rejected it in the referendum on April 24, 2004.

A small but influential number of Turks have an ambivalent attitude toward the EU. At the time there was a growing camp of EU skeptics who suggested that Turkey's interests lay elsewhere. They were concerned about a loss of sovereignty and believed that EU membership will force Turkey to forfeit its rights in the Aegean. No matter how seriously Turkey tries to meet the Copenhagen criteria, they maintained that ultimately Europe would decide that it really does not want to include 70 million Muslims in its Christian community.

* * *

Track Two endeavors are continuing. For example, the Greek-Turkish Forum facilitates discussions on delimitation of the continental shelf, territorial waters, and air space.[10] The Western Policy Center organizes conferences on security in the eastern Mediterranean. The European Commission supports training and journalist exchanges organized by the European Centre for Common Ground. The Greek-Turkish Media Dialogue works with media executives from the largest conglomerates in Greece and Turkey. It runs training workshops on journalism ethics and conflict resolution reporting. Regarding media content, it organizes article exchanges and joint production of radio and television documentaries.

In 1999, I conducted a series of Track Two training programs for U.S. embassy staff in Ankara and Athens. An enterprising young cultural affairs specialist started an inventory of Track Two activities. His notes evolved into a database, which proved invaluable in monitoring the virtual explosion of cooperative civil society activities.

Grossman urged me to discontinue my involvement in Greek-Turkish Track Two activities. The earthquakes had brought about a surge in both people-to-people and official contacts. American involvement, either via management assistance or project finance, was no longer necessary. Grossman felt that Greeks and Turks had reached a critical mass of activity and could carry on without the assistance of third parties.

For a career foreign service officer, Grossman has a rare combination of skills. His steely-eyed realism is tempered by an idealistic commitment to human rights. Grossman is also a skillful diplomat who is expert at managing the bureaucracy to get things done. In addition, he has a keen intellectual curiosity and a willingness to experiment with new ideas.

Grossman took a special interest in a Greek-Turkish academic consortium that was working on a "shared history" of the Ottoman Empire's final years. Scholars were studying the September 1922 "Burning of Smyrna," as it is known by Greeks, or the "Fire of Izmir," as called by Turks. For Greeks, the "Anatolian Catastrophe" signaled the demise of Greek claims and the final death of Greek imperial aspirations. Turks view the event as part of Turkey's painful birth from the ashes of the collapsed Ottoman Empire. On April 23, 1923, the Republic of Turkey was formed by Mustafa Kemal—"Ataturk," the father of all Turks.

The shared history project brought Greek and Turkish scholars together to exchange research materials, record oral histories, write parallel renditions of events, and, when possible, coauthor papers. To launch the initiative, I invited scholars from Sabanci, Panteion, Aegean, and Yannina Universities to a "Seminar on the Construction of National Memory in Greece and Turkey."

The shared history approach is based on the conviction that today's conflicts are often rooted in the past, and that analysis of historical events can enhance better understanding between communities in conflict. It occurred to Grossman that the shared history methodology could also be used to foster a Track Two dialogue between the bitterest of rivals—Turks and Armenians.

I would rely heavily on my Greek-Turkish and Cypriot Track Two experience during every phase of the Track Two dialogue involving Turks and Armenians. Relations with prominent Turks would prove invaluable. So would important lessons learned on techniques for developing a Track Two endeavor. To maximize its positive contribution, Track Two should:

- Seek to influence policy through close coordination with officials, including mediators as well as officials at headquarters and in the field.

- Emphasize efforts to shape public opinion by involving a broad cross-section of civil society.
- Adapt strategies when outside events affect the context of activities.
- Foster human relations between project participants, which are critical to overcoming problems that inevitably arise.
- Secure adequate project finance from a variety of sources.
- Keep a detailed record of activities.

Notes

1. Remarks by Richard C. Holbrooke, Brussels, November 1997.
2. Conference Statement, Oslo, July 2, 1998.
3. Statement by President Juncker of Luxembourg, December 1998.
4. *Turkish Daily News,* December 14, 1998.
5. Interview with author, August 6, 2003.
6. John Sitilides, "Greek-Turkish Relations: Assessing Opportunities," *Western Policy Center,* March 30, 2000.
7. Statement by George Papandreou, Taksim Roundtable, October 3, 1999.
8. John Sitilides, "Greek-Turkish Relations: The Geopolitical Context," *Western Policy Center,* November 6, 1999.
9. FBIS, Doc. ID #GMP 20010401000065.
10. Statement by the Greek-Turkish Forum, Issues in the Aegean: Openings and Possibilities, June 23, 2000.

2

FIRST CONTACT

Historical differences between Turks and Armenians are compounded by the more recent conflict between Armenians and Turkey's ethnic brethren in Azerbaijan. In 1994, Russia negotiated an uneasy cease-fire to the fratricidal war, but no final peace agreement was reached.

Ethnic violence in Azerbaijan over Nagorno-Karabakh was more brutal and bloody than in any other post-Soviet republic. Though Azeri nationalists threaten to take back territory by force, Karabakh Armenians enjoy vast military superiority. In a matter of minutes Armenian S-300 missiles could destroy Baku and wipe out Azerbaijan's energy industry. U.S. companies have a big stake in the international energy consortium. By 2007, more than one million barrels of oil a day are planned to be transported via pipeline from Baku to the Turkish port of Ceyhan on the Mediterranean.

Not only do the republics of Turkey and Azerbaijan share economic interests, the links between Anatolian and Azeri Turks are deeply rooted in history. Azeris were among the "Young Turks" who led Turkey's nationalist movement between 1908 and 1918. Though Ataturk opposed expansionism, an ultranationalist movement evolved exalting Turkishness from the Aegean to Central Asia. "Turanism" vowed to unite Turks in a pan-Turkic federation. During the Cold War, Turkish politicians promised the salvation of enslaved Turks behind the iron curtain. Interest focused on Azerbaijan because of its proximity and oil wealth. When Azerbaijan became independent following the demise of the Soviet Union, President Abulfez Elcibey pronounced, "We are two states but one nation."[1]

Though Turkey recognized Armenia after the Soviet Union collapsed, diplomatic relations were never established. With the outbreak of hostilities over Nagorno-Karabakh, Turkey closed its border with Armenia and expressed solidarity with Azerbaijan by imposing an economic blockade.

* * *

Armenia desires normal relations with Turkey without preconditions. However, Ankara refuses to establish diplomatic ties until Azerbaijan's territorial integrity is restored. It also demands that Armenians abandon their efforts to affirm the Armenian genocide by seeking resolutions in parliaments around the world. In coordination with the worldwide Armenian Diaspora, Armenia's president Robert Kocharian made recognition of the "Armenian genocide" a key foreign policy objective.

Kocharian was upset with the OSCE's plan to hold its 1999 summit in Istanbul. The OSCE includes fifty-three countries and acts through consensus. But when one member state objects, a provision exists for decision-making by "consensus minus one." Armenia's foreign minister, Vartan Oskanian, knew he could not block the Istanbul summit, but he saw an opportunity to raise objections and put pressure on Turkey.

Circumventing Armenia's ambassador to the United States, Oskanian asked Van Krikorian to undertake discussions with the State Department. Van is a leading figure in the Armenian-American community with a reputation as able lawyer and a tough negotiator. The Armenian archbishop once described Van to me as a "good Armenian." When I asked what that meant, he explained, "Van spent his life seeking justice for the Armenian people."[2]

While a student at Georgetown University, Van Krikorian filed a Freedom of Information Act (FOIA) request for records relating to a State Department article on Armenian terrorism. Published in 1982, the article included a "note" that stated that because the historical record was "ambiguous," the Department did not "endorse allegations that the Turkish government committed a genocide against the Armenian people." The note contradicted President Ronald Reagan's 1981 executive order recognizing the genocide of Armenians. In 1986, Van sued the department, claiming that it had exhibited "bad faith" by failing to fully comply with its FOIA requirements. Seven years later, the U.S. Court of Appeals for the District of Columbia ruled in his favor, finding that the State Department had indeed failed to provide all documents related to the memo.[3]

By successfully taking on the U.S. government, Van became a star in the Armenian-American community. As a boy, Van was founder and president of his local Dashnak youth organization. The Armenian Revolutionary Federation, otherwise called the Dashnak Party, includes the most radical, belligerent, and ultranationalist Armenians. After interning at the Armenian Assembly of America, Van joined its staff, became a board member, and was elected chairman of the board in 1998. Over the years, Van had his hand in every piece of legislation concerning Armenia. By his own admission, Van "got pretty good at counting votes on Capitol Hill."[4]

As Assistant Secretary of State for European Affairs, Marc Grossman's portfolio covered the Organization for Security and Cooperation in Europe, including summit arrangements. When Van visited the State Department to discuss plans for the meeting in Istanbul, he called on Grossman. Van knew that he could make himself a nuisance, but that efforts to block the meeting would ultimately be unsuccessful. Grossman suggested he pursue another course. Instead of trying to disrupt the summit, he urged Van to seek a substantive dialogue with Turks. The State Department had just hired me as a consultant; Grossman promised to introduce Van to the department's new conflict resolution specialist—the "shared history guy."

Grossman was in New York a few weeks later, and we arranged to meet at a café around the corner from Van's law office. Grossman recounted his first encounter with Van. In 1992, Van Krikorian and Hrair Hovnanian, an Armenian construction tycoon from New Jersey, visited Turkey at the request of Armenia's president, Levon Ter-Petrossian, to explore a business venture at the Turkish port of Trabzon on the Black Sea. During their discussion with the foreign minister, the Armenians expressed their hope that expanded commercial contact between Armenians and Turks would help normalize relations between the two governments. As a goodwill gesture, the foreign minister told Van and Hovnanian that special arrangements would be made for them to cross the border from Turkey into Armenia. But when they got to the bridge, the travelers were detained by Turkish border police. The guard told Van, "We have information that you are the number one enemy of the Turkish state."[5] Van relayed a message about their predicament to the American embassy in Ankara where Grossman was Deputy Chief of Mission. Grossman helped secure their release; Van was deeply grateful.

Grossman and I met Van in his elegant glass and chrome-plated office. I described the shared history approach and discussed Greek-Turkish Track Two activities. Van was adamant that there was only one version of history and that the Armenian genocide was an indisputable fact. He warned us that any distortion would only make the situation worse. Though I thought this was bluster, I later learned about the deep divisions in the Armenian-American community and the terror tactics of some Armenians. Hard-line Armenians oppose any contact with Turks until Turkey admits the genocide, pays reparations, and returns territory in "Western Armenia."

In the 1970s and 1980s, Armenian terrorists organized cells such as the Armenian Secret Army for the Liberation of Armenia (ASALA) and assassinated thirty-four Turkish diplomats. Mehmet Baydar, Turkey's consul

general in San Francisco, was the first casualty. He was invited to a dinner by an Armenian-American and, after being seated at the table, was
murdered in cold blood. Prominent figures in Turkey's Foreign Service,
including the country's ambassadors to France, Austria, Yugoslavia, and
the Vatican, were also assassinated. ASALA thought the tactic would draw
attention to their campaign of genocide recognition. But it merely en-
raged Turkish civil servants and hardened Turkish public opinion.

After hearing Van's "red lines," we agreed to move forward with a meeting between Turks and Armenians. Van arranged for me to interview Robert Kaloosdian, chairman of the Armenian National Institute, who offered
his help arranging Armenian participation. Neither Van nor Kaloosdian
showed much interest in developing friendship between Turks and Armenians. To them, reconciliation was a zero sum gain that could only be
achieved through Ankara's admission of the genocide.

* * *

I was not surprised by their hard-line. Parties always assume maxi-
malist positions at the outset of a structured dialogue. I expected the
same from Turks and started seeking a suitable Turkish partner. I was introduced to the Turkish History Foundation. Its director is an old leftist
named Orhan Silier. Our first meeting was a harbinger of difficulties to
come.

Silier and his wife were visiting New York and I invited them to my
home for cocktails. It was a bitterly cold evening and, unable to find a
taxi, they had taken a long walk through Central Park. When she took
off her coat, Silier's wife went to light a cigarette. As politely as possible,
I told her there was no smoking in my residence. She got very agitated
and put on her coat to go outside into the snowy night. Upon return, she
was hostile and argumentative.

Like Van, Silier also had his "red lines." We exchanged many email
messages on arrangements for a "Seminar on the Construction of Armenian and Turkish National Identity in the Early Twentieth Century."
After much back and forth, we finalized an agenda focusing on scholarly
work in Turkey and Armenia. The seminar would also assess the avail-
ability of research materials, including documents in Turkish, Armenian,
and international archives. We disagreed, however, on the definition of
national identity. He believed that the seminar should only address Armenians in the Ottoman Empire and modern-day Armenia. Since most
Armenians live in the Diaspora, I maintained that we should include
them as well.

Though Silier ultimately agreed, we reached an impasse selecting
seminar participants. He proposed an accomplished group of Turkish
academicians, which included some nationalist historians. However, he

strongly objected to Dr. Rouben Adalian, director of the Armenian National Institute. Adalian was author and editor of many publications, including the *Encyclopedia of Genocide,* the *Armenian Genocide Resource Guide,* and the *Guide to the Armenian Genocide in the U.S. Archives (1915–18).* Though I appreciated Silier's concern about Adalian, I felt that his participation was important. I was prepared to discuss any and all concerns but I reserved the right to make decisions, which I felt were in the project's interests.

Recalling Kaloosdian's inflexible position, I had little choice but to insist on Adalian's inclusion. I knew that excluding him would cause the whole endeavor to fall apart. I was concerned about blemishing my record of success and losing Grossman's trust. Dealing with Silier, I came to realize that the Turkish History Foundation had too many constraints and would never be a suitable partner for a constructive and results-oriented Track Two program. I apologized for any inconvenience and informed Silier that I was canceling plans for the meeting.

* * *

I learned three important lessons from my discussions with the History Foundation. First, it is essential to retain control over decision-making during the sensitive start-up of a Track Two endeavor. Second, initial meetings should be convened at a neutral site. Third, it is much easier to overcome differences when there is institutional familiarity and a precedent of good working relations. My failure also served as a reminder of the need to persevere.

The setback made me even more determined to bring Turks and Armenians together. Helena Finn encouraged me to approach Sabanci University. My effort to involve Sabanci could not have come at a worse time. The Sabanci family had recently experienced a terrible tragedy. Sakip Sabanci had spoken out against the cycle of repression and violence involving Kurds in southeastern Turkey. A gunman had walked into the office of Sakip's younger brother and assassinated him. Sabanci University is a private university supported financially by the Sabanci family. Ahmet Evin, dean at the School of Social Sciences, was at his wits' end launching a new department and managing the Greek-Turkish task forces. At first he declined to get involved. Helena Finn reached out to Ahmet, and I flew to Istanbul in order to persuade him.

The "Discussion between Armenian and Turkish Scholars and Civil Society Representatives" was finally convened at the Diplomatic Academy of Vienna on June 10, 2000. Evin was joined by Halil Berktay, an accomplished historian with the uncanny ability to speak with authority and at great length on seemingly every subject. The other Turkish participant was Ozdem Sanberk, a likable fellow who had just retired from the Turkish foreign ministry and become director of the Turkish Economic and Social Studies Foundation (TESEV). Ozdem was known as a subtle and sophisticated diplomat while serving as Turkey's ambassador to the United Kingdom and undersecretary of foreign affairs. He is an experienced bureaucrat who learned the importance of hierarchy during his many years in Turkey's Foreign Ministry.

Rouben Adalian, Khachig Tololyan, an affable Armenian-American from Wesleyan University, and Tevan Poghosyan, who directs the International Center for Human Development (ICHD) in Yerevan, also participated. I invited Joe Montville, a seasoned Track Two professional, to sit in as a "resource person."

Consistent with classic Track Two methodology, I arranged separate preworkshop discussions with the Turks and Armenians. Preworkshop discussions are essential for building confidence between delegation members and for establishing the *bona fides* of the facilitator. We discussed expectations, the agenda, and ground rules.

During my opening remarks, I noticed that interaction was stiff and uncomfortable. When we went around the table to introduce ourselves, Berktay stunned everyone by referring to the "Armenian genocide." Given the importance of acknowledgment, his reference put the Armenians at ease and, as a turning point in the meeting, dramatically changed the dynamics of our discussion.

Following the example of the Greek-Turkish shared history project, we discussed potential areas for collaborative scholarship. We also discussed Turkish and Armenian official records, encyclopedias, and textbooks. We reviewed the status of Turkish-Armenian relations and explored prospects for contact and cooperation between Turkish and Armenian civil society representatives. The meeting went well.

That evening we attended a concert of Bruckner's *Grosse Messe*. On our way out of the old church, we coincidentally ran into Turkey's ambassador to Austria. He was surprised to see Ozdem, his old colleague from the foreign ministry, with a group of Armenians. "What are you doing in Vienna?" he asked. Ozdem adroitly responded, "We came for the concert." After the performance, we dined at one of Vienna's finest eateries and laughed together about the chance encounter.

The next morning we reconvened to review progress and discuss next steps. Ozdem started the discussion by graciously inviting Tevan to Turkey. They discussed potential areas of cooperation between TESEV and ICHD. Sabanci University agreed to act as a clearinghouse of information on scholarly cooperation. We would discuss the feasibility, sequence, and timing of activities at our next meeting in Istanbul.

The mere fact that Armenians and Turks were talking was a huge step forward. Moreover, they had identified topics to work on, committed their institutions to specific activities, and agreed to meet again. Grossman was delighted with the outcome. Always hard to please, even Van was satisfied.

Though the Vienna meeting was no secret, we agreed on the need for discretion. However, within days of his return to Istanbul, Berktay gave a long interview confirming the meeting and referring to the "Armenian genocide." His widely reported comments generated a swarm of controversy. Berktay received death threats and hundreds of hate messages. Sabanci was besieged with demands for his dismissal, but held its ground invoking the principle of academic independence.

Controversy was further fueled by events in Washington, D.C. It is customary for the president of the United States to issue a statement on the April 24 Remembrance Day of the Armenian genocide. President Clinton stated, "The United States fully supports the efforts of Armenia and its neighbors to make lasting peace with one another and to begin an era of security and cooperation in the Caucasus region. We encourage any and all dialogue between citizens of the region that hastens reconciliation and understanding."[6] Dissatisfied with his remarks, members of Congress introduced House Resolution 596 calling for the president to use the term "genocide" in characterizing the 1915 massacres of Armenians in what is now eastern Turkey.

Though Ozdem was representing his think tank, he stayed in close contact with the foreign ministry and was always deferential to the state. Ozdem insisted that no activities were possible so long as Turkey remained under threat and duress. Track Two was suspended pending an outcome to events on Capitol Hill.

Notes

1. Cited by Dogu Ergil in an interview with the author, August 5, 2003.
2. Discussion with the author, New York, November 20, 2001.
3. *Journal of the Armenian Bar Association*, February 1993.
4. Interview with the author, July 10, 2003.
5. Interview with the author, July 10, 2003.
6. The White House, April 24, 2000.

3

LEGISLATING HISTORY

House Resolution 596—the "Armenian Genocide Resolution"—was introduced in September 2000. As a presidential candidate, Bill Clinton pledged to commemorate the Armenian genocide. However, the Clinton administration opposed the bill. It believed that passage of the resolution would have serious negative consequences for U.S.-Turkish relations and that a fallout with Turkey would hurt U.S. national security interests.

The United States and Turkey have enjoyed a special relationship for decades. As the eastern flank of NATO, Turkey was an invaluable ally during the Cold War. Beginning with the Korean conflict, U.S. and Turkish forces served side by side for half a century. In Korea, the U.S. was impressed with the military capability and the capacity for sacrifice of Turkish troops. Turkey saw NATO as a bridge to the West and took her Alliance commitments seriously. Turkish bases became NATO facilities; U.S. nuclear weapons were also based in Turkey.

More than ever, Turkey was an indispensable ally during the 1991 Gulf War. President Turgut Ozal vigorously supported America's campaign to oppose Saddam's takeover of Kuwait. At Washington's request, Ozal closed the border with Iraq and shut down Iraq's oil pipeline to the Mediterranean. Turkey paid a steep price for its cooperation. UN sanctions on Iraq cost the Turkish economy an estimated $40 billion.

Turkey participated in the 1991 Gulf War despite domestic opposition and concerns about regional instability. When a million Iraqi Kurds fled Saddam Hussein's reprisals, many came across the border. The U.S. and Turkey worked together to address the humanitarian emergency through Operation Provide Comfort. In addition, Turkey hosted American and British planes participating in Operation Northern Watch enforcing a no-fly zone in Iraq's airspace north of the 36th parallel and guarding against renewed aggression by Saddam.

Washington also appreciates Turkey's extensive ties to Israel. So do powerful pro-Israel lobby groups in the United States. Israel provides Turkey with critical technology to modernize its U.S.-acquired Abrams tanks and F-16 jet fighters. In return, Israeli pilots use Turkey's airspace for training missions. There are also extensive trade and cultural contacts. Israeli avocados are for sale in Turkey's markets, and Israeli tourists are often found at nightspots in Bodrum and at other resorts on the Turkish coast.

At the same time, Turkey maintains good relations with the Palestinians. Palestine and Egypt were incorporated into the Ottoman Empire during the early sixteenth century when the caliphate was moved to Istanbul. The blood of Turkish and Palestinian forces flowed together when they fought side by side in Gaza during the First World War. As the only member of the Organization of the Islamic Conference with ties to Israel, Turkey envisions itself with a role in the Middle East peace process.

U.S. and Turkish commercial interests are also closely connected. The Turkish government is helping to finance the construction of the oil and gas pipeline from Baku via Georgia to the Turkish port of Ceyhan on the Mediterranean. The Commerce Department considers Turkey a major emerging market; Turkey purchases $6 billion each year in American agricultural goods and defense and aerospace technologies.

To Turks, the U.S. is more than an ally. The United States and Turkey are strategic partners bound together by shared interests and a history of common endeavor. Loyalty—"Sadakat"—is a cherished value in Turkish society. For Turks, loyalty is continuous and unwavering. It implies reciprocity, sacrifice, and commitment. There is nothing more treasured than a reliable friend. Turks were incredulous that the U.S. Congress would blame Turkey for events during the Ottoman period. Moreover, many Turks believe the events never occurred. The term "genocide" invokes horrible images of the Nazi death camps. They find it incomprehensible that their forefathers could have ever participated in such barbarous acts.

The administration's opposition to H.R. 596 was laid out in a letter from Secretary of State Madeleine Albright and Secretary of Defense William Cohen to House Speaker Dennis Hastert (R-IL). They wrote that the bill would adversely impact "American national security interests in the Eastern Mediterranean, Middle East, the Caucasus and Central Asia."[1] Upon his return from Washington where he was "participating in the Administration's continuing efforts against H.R. 596," Robert Pearson, America's ambassador to Turkey, said, "The U.S. government believes that passage of the resolution would hinder, not encourage, progress on regional and bilateral issues important to both the U.S. and Turkey. The U.S. gov-

ernment sees Turkey as a friend and key ally in a critical region. We want
to work with Turkey to achieve our common objectives."[2]

Preferential treatment of Turkey was not unique to the Clinton administration. The special relationship has been nurtured ever since the administration of President Dwight Eisenhower. In 2002, Deputy Secretary
of Defense Paul Wolfowitz affirmed that "It is the great good fortune of
the United States, of the NATO alliance, of the West, and indeed of the
world, that occupying this most important crossroads we have one of
our strongest, most reliable and most self-reliant allies."[3]

Turkey organized a vigorous campaign to defeat H.R. 596. Gunduz
Aktan, a retired diplomat who served as Turkey's ambassador to the UN
Human Rights Commission, presented Ankara's case in Washington. He
maintained, "When it comes to qualifying events 85 years ago in the Ottoman Empire, Turks will never accept them as genocide. We certainly
consider them terrible tragic events, but they do not fall within the definition of genocide accepted under international humanitarian law."[4] In
a threatening manner, Gunduz warned of reprisals against the U.S. if the
resolution was adopted. His warning did not sit well with the Congress.

Gunduz is a controversial figure who played a pivotal role in TARC.
He resigned from the Foreign Service after being unfairly accused by the
administration of Prime Minister Tansu Ciller of financial improprieties
associated with the purchase of the Turkish residence on Lake Geneva.
Recognizing that politicians come and go, Gunduz engineered a comeback
by aligning himself with anti-Western elements in the security establishment. He fought against human rights reforms as Turkey's ambassador to
the UN Human Rights Commission. Arguing that language implies national identity and national identity leads to demands for independence,
he was bitterly opposed to liberalizing Kurdish language broadcasts and
education. Over his career, Gunduz has capitalized on Turkey's insecuri-
ties lobbying against EU membership, Cyprus unification, and rapprochement with Armenia. Ilter Turkmen commented, "When you feel insecure,
everything is a danger."[5] Gunduz is an ambitious man who wants to be
a figure in public opinion. Once a week, he publishes a commentary in
Radikal and often appears on Turkey's marathon television talk shows.
He sees himself as the Henry Kissinger of Turkey—well regarded, highly
respected, and frequently consulted.

Like many Turks, Gunduz refers to events in the early twentieth century as a "mutual tragedy." An Armenian Atrocities Monument has been
erected in Igdir, a town in Turkey near the Armenian border. Four inter-
locking scimitars, which can be seen across the border, commemorate
the mass murder of Turks by Armenians. Ordinary Turks have no idea
what happened to Armenians living in the Ottoman Empire. After the
evacuation of Armenian lands, there is no official record of their pres-

ence. Armenians living in Kars are called "Yerli," which literally means "man of the place." Dogu Ergil is a tenured member of the political science faculty at Ankara University. While pursuing graduate studies in the U.S., an Armenian-American classmate confronted him. "Your grandfather slaughtered mine." Ergil did not know the history. He went to the library and was shocked to find a huge volume of literature on the predicament of Armenians during the twilight of the Ottoman Empire.[6]

Turks know of the hardships they endured during the final years of the Ottoman Empire. After the British refused to establish an alliance with the Ottoman Empire, Germany sponsored two million Ottoman troops to fight in World War I. They were ultimately defeated on every front— from Europe to Iran, the Caucasus, and the Suez Canal. However, the official version of Turkish history refuses to acknowledge defeat. It says that the Axis powers surrendered and Turkey was forced to follow suit. At the beginning of the war, the Ottoman Empire spanned 4.3 million km^2. By war's end, it was reduced to 770,000 km^2.

* * *

Most Armenians have little sympathy for the historical suffering of Turks. Armenians strongly dispute Turkish claims regarding the magnitude and scope of events, their context and intended effect, and the identities and affiliations of their perpetrators. They believe there was a master plan to purge the Ottoman Empire of its Armenian minority, which culminated in the deportation and death of up to 1.5 million Armenians. Ergil asked, "What happened to the Armenian homes and why didn't Armenians return after the war?"[7]

In affirming the Armenian genocide, Armenians point to "sources of unquestioned integrity and credibility," including official dispatches from Ambassador Henry M. Morgenthau and cables from consular offices. Morgenthau reported, "When the Turkish authorities gave the orders for these deportations, they were giving the death warrant to the whole race. They understood this well in their conversations with me; they made no particular effort to conceal the fact."[8] From 1894 to 1922, the *New York Times* included more than a thousand reports of Armenian "massacres."[9] Rafael Lemkin, an author of the Convention on the Prevention and Punishment of the Crime of Genocide, described genocide as "what happened to the Armenians."[10]

Ankara believes that international action on genocide recognition is an obsession of the Armenian Diaspora. They point to Robert Kocharian's statement that "During more than 70 years of Soviet rule, official Yerevan never dealt with this issue. The Armenian Diaspora has always been actively engaged in seeking recognition. Diaspora Armenians are those people who were victims of those events, or more correctly their descendants. They can't remain indifferent toward this matter."[11] Turkish officials insist that efforts by the Diaspora impede progress and obstruct regional cooperation; Ankara is convinced that Armenians in Armenia have more practical concerns. Though the Armenian genocide is the central reference point of Diaspora Armenians, tragedy touched the life of every Armenian and has forged a collective memory that transcends national boundaries. Every year on Remembrance Day, more than a million Armenians from Armenia and around the world make a pilgrimage to the Memorial. To Van Krikorian and most Armenians, "The Armenian genocide is fundamental to who we are."[12]

It is predictable that Armenians in Armenia place great importance on opening the border with Turkey. After all, it is they who suffer from Turkey's embargo on normal travel and trade. Young Armenians have limited prospects in landlocked, isolated, and impoverished Armenia. About 1.5 million Armenians have emigrated since independence in 1988. No Armenian would, however, deny the genocide in exchange for opening the borders. When Kocharian became president of Armenia in 1998, he made genocide recognition a central part of his foreign policy. Reflecting the view of every Armenian, Vartan Oskanian maintains that "Memory does not heal by denial. Truthfully assuming responsibility is a precondition for rebuilding trust."[13]

* * *

Even U.S. officials who opposed H.R. 596 acknowledged the terrible tragedy that befell Armenians and felt special sympathy for descendants of survivors. In the final days of the 106th Congress, just before the November election, broad bipartisan support for H.R. 596 was building. The House International Relations Committee moved the bill out of committee by a vote of 24 to 11. It looked increasingly likely that the resolution would be considered by the full U.S. House of Representatives.

Turkey intensified its diplomatic offensive and warned of dire consequences. Defense Chief General Huseyn Kivrikoglu cancelled a long-scheduled trip to Washington. The Turkish Grand National Assembly threatened to scuttle Operation Northern Watch, which requires an extension every six months. Ankara insisted that passage of the resolution would destroy any hope of normalizing relations between Armenia and Turkey. To prove the point, it implemented a policy refusing to grant visas at the Istanbul airport to Armenian passport holders.

Though Turkish officials insisted they would not negotiate under duress, prospects for passage of the resolution created an opening for serious dialogue. Turkey sent out discreet feelers. Stephen R. Sestanovich, the assistant secretary of state for the Newly Independent States, and Dan Fried, former U.S. ambassador to Poland and Sestanovich's deputy, held discussions with Turkish officials about a truth and reconciliation process. The State Department also urged me to open a channel to the government of Turkey. A U.S. official arranged for me to meet a representative from the Turkish embassy at a coffee shop on Dupont Circle. The Turk assured me that I would find him in the crowd. He would be wearing a fedora hat.

He appeared at the appointed hour and asked that our discussions be treated confidentially. He told me that he was acting on direct instructions of the foreign minister without the knowledge of Turkey's ambassador to the United States. Ankara had deep reservations about my involvement, he warned. My human rights activism on behalf of the Kurds had not escaped notice by Turkey's National Intelligence Organization. Despite concerns, Turkey was prepared to work with me. The U.S. government had made clear that I would lead the Turkish-Armenian dialogue. To ensure no misunderstanding, he repeated several times, "My minister is committed to a successful truth and reconciliation process."

Sestanovich and Fried are experienced diplomats. Over several hours, I briefed them on the Vienna meeting and the Greek-Turkish shared history project. Both saw value in a Track Two process, particularly in lieu of continued State Department involvement in what promised to be a difficult and drawn-out affair.

Fried demonstrated a keen intellectual curiosity in Track Two. He focused on shared history and educational reform as tools for peacebuilding. In addition to the review of Turkish and Armenian textbooks, I described other efforts to identify negative stereotyping and eliminate nationalist messages in academic curricula. In 1996, Bogazici University worked with Greek educators to review academic textbooks used in northern Thrace. In addition, the Center for Democracy and Reconciliation in Southeastern Europe undertook an extensive effort on "History and History Teaching." Starting in December 1999, the center established a History Education Committee to assess sensitive and controversial issues in history education. The committee focused on Byzantine and Ottoman legacies, and the role of educational systems fueling nationalism in the Balkans. It assessed the educational system in several countries and the extent of government control over textbooks.

I was impressed by Fried's long-term perspective. Of course he was focused on the immediate challenges of launching a Turkish-Armenian dialogue. But he also understood the importance of a patient approach, as well as the need to engage different sectors of society in altering national perceptions. It would take time to change the demonization of Turks by Armenians and the stereotyping of Armenians by Turks. Fried's capacity to see the big picture garnered my immediate respect.

Once again, Kocharian and Oskanian turned to Van. In his meetings with Sestanovich and Fried, Van emphasized that the congressional resolution was nonnegotiable. It was a matter for the U.S. Congress, and ought not to get in the way of dialogue between Turkey and Armenia. However, Van had too much experience in legislative affairs to put all his eggs in one basket. Passage of the resolution could still go awry.

Van confirmed that Armenia was prepared to participate in a truth and reconciliation process. He was, however, absolutely inflexible on one point. Its purpose was not to explore the truth of the Armenian genocide. That fact was beyond question. Turkish officials objected to Van's precondition. They also insisted that they would not negotiate under duress. As long as H.R. 596 was hanging over their heads, no progress was possible.

The Turkish government tends to respond defensively to issues that are imposed on it. When faced with a complex problem, Ankara rarely demonstrates the vision and capacity for a well-coordinated strategy. Turks are good administrators when it comes to running daily affairs, but less skillful at developing a nuanced proactive policy that requires vision and flexibility. In Turkey, the state seeks obedience, not creativity, from its citizens. Democratic plurality and individual initiative are undeveloped; Ankara distrusts Track Two.

Despite their skepticism, Turkish officials ultimately agreed to a Track Two truth and reconciliation process. Ankara was motivated by the desire to avoid a setback in U.S.-Turkish relations. They also knew that a messy dustup with Armenia would hurt Turkey's goal of joining the European Union (EU). Continued tensions with Armenia would also allow Russia, Turkey's historic rival in the Black Sea region, to exert greater influence in the South Caucasus. It was agreed that the U.S. would ensure the integrity of a truth and reconciliation process by stewarding its early stages.

I cautioned Sestanovich and Fried that significant resources would be required for an officially sanctioned initiative. The South African Truth and Reconciliation Commission employed a thousand people and cost $18 million each year. I advised them to keep expectations low and set realistic sights. To move the process forward, a well-respected and adequately resourced NGO would be necessary. I proposed the U.S. Institute of Peace (USIP).

Van wanted to be sure that the Turks were serious. He and Sestanovich suggested that the secretary of state send letters to the Turkish and Armenian foreign ministers spelling out a work plan and precise goals. Both Van and State Department officials separately sought my counsel in drafting the correspondence. It was finally agreed that Albright would send a general letter proposing the process to Turkey's Foreign Minister

Ismail Cem and Oskanian. She would attach the copy of another letter sent to USIP detailing terms of reference, methodology, and the time-table for deliverables.

Then lightning struck. Just as H.R. 596 was about to come up for a vote by the House of Representatives, President Clinton called Hastert and asked him to pull the resolution. The president invoked national se-curity concerns about terrorism and emphasized the need for Turkey's assistance in meeting threats to American interests in the Middle East.

Armenians were stunned by the eleventh-hour demise of the resolu-tion. They had expended enormous effort and resources. Van took the news especially hard. He anticipated that efforts to restart a dialogue would also collapse. However, Sestanovich and Fried persevered. The Turks had always maintained they would not negotiate under duress. With the res-olution off the table, U.S. officials approached Ankara anew. They were surprised by the response. Withdrawal of H.R. 596 triggered Ankara's in-terest in addressing Turkish-Armenian issues "once and for all."

Meanwhile in Turkey, a plethora of Armenian-related proposals was put forward. The TGNA suggested a parliamentary commission. The In-stitute for Central Asian Strategic Studies called for opening the Otto-man archives. Sukru Elekdag, a former ambassador to the United States, worked with Bilkent University to establish a commission of historians.

Though interest in Turkish-Armenian rapprochement was encourag-ing, there was risk associated with the proliferation of initiatives. Too many could diffuse the impact of a commission. There were also questions of good faith. Many of the Turkish proposals failed to involve Armenians. To be credible, the truth and reconciliation process would have to be a joint effort. U.S. officials believed that a single dialogue framework, with private participants in close contact with Turkish and Armenian author-ities, was preferable.

At the State Department's request, I visited Turkey to assess the cur-rent climate concerning Turkish-Armenian relations and to explore op-portunities for Track Two. Most Turks were favorably disposed toward NGO activities involving Turks and Armenians. A few days after my visit, Gunduz wrote, "It's no secret that the U.S. State Department has been suggesting that the two sides should come together. There are reports that certain Turkish, Armenian and U.S. nongovernmental organizations will launch joint programs to tackle and debate the historical, legal and psy-chological aspects of the issue."[14]

But how would Armenians see the prospect after their setback on Capitol Hill? On November 6, Sestanovich met Kocharian in Yerevan. Kocharian was in a foul mood and railed against Clinton's betrayal. He was so cantankerous that participants in the meeting thought Kocharian was still suffering the aftereffects from his oral surgery. The president had just returned from a visit to his dentist in Paris.

* * *

With the Armenian Diaspora pledging to reintroduce the resolution as soon as the next Congress convened, I accelerated plans to visit Armenia and Turkey. Helena Finn became my trusted advisor. She and I had met at an embassy reception in 1998. Subsequently serving as the Principal Deputy Assistant Secretary in the Bureau of Educational and Cultural Affairs, Helena encouraged me to "Go to Ankara first and have an Embassy briefing. Then I recommend that you sound Turks out for their suggestions on possible approaches for track two conflict resolution."[15]

I met Pearson late in the afternoon on December 23. The genocide resolution had been tabled during Pearson's first days as America's new ambassador to Turkey. From the day of his arrival, Turkish officials put pressure on Pearson about the bill. Though Pearson welcomed people-to-people contacts, he was wary of Track Two. Pearson believed that problems between governments should be resolved between government representatives.

Mike Lemmon, America's ambassador to Armenia, had a different view of Track Two. Lemmon was an activist who pursued his official duties with exuberance and passion. He pledged his unequivocal support for Track Two. Though an outsider to the State Department, I knew that support from Washington was not enough. It was imperative to involve U.S. officials in Turkey and Armenia. I vowed to consult regularly with embassy staff, and to keep Pearson and Lemmon abreast of developments.

On December 27, I sent Sestanovich and Fried my trip report and proposed what was referred to at the time as an "Armenian-Turkish History Commission." I envisioned a comprehensive Track Two program with the commission at its core and involving other sectors of society. My memo described a media strategy, joint economic development initiatives, collaborative cultural events, academic cooperation, youth exchanges, and training in conflict resolution for local government officials from Armenian and Turkish border provinces. The original description of activities looked a lot like the *Track Two Program on Turkey and the Caucasus*—which would be finalized six months later.

I feared that the window of opportunity for Track Two would soon shut. Pursuant to its 1987 resolution, the European parliament reaffirmed that if Turkey wanted to join the EU it would have to recognize that the events of 1915 constituted genocide. The resolution also called on Turkey to lift its economic blockade of Armenia.

As a result of the European parliament resolution, an increasing number of Turks were coming to see the European Union as a community of values to which Muslim Turks were simply not welcome. As a result, many

Turks feel rejected and treated like second-class citizens. Turkey was insulted to see former Warsaw Pact countries on a fast track to EU membership while Turkey, a long-time NATO member and friend of the West, was shunted aside without so much as a starting date for negotiations on its candidacy.

On February 1, 2001, the French parliament adopted a resolution simply stating that "France publicly recognizes the Armenian genocide of 1915." Turkey responded by recalling its ambassador to France and annulling two commercial transactions, each worth about $200 million, with the French companies Thales and Alcatel. Turkey's minister of defense warned that the resolution would have bearing on the evaluation of pending French bids to supply military equipment. When Gunduz called to inquire about arrangements for a brainstorming session later that spring, he told me that Turkish business associations were organizing a boycott of French products. "California wines are just as good. Your boycott is good for American business," I chided.

Why does Turkey react so strongly to international recognition of the genocide? Turks refuse to acknowledge the genocide because acknowledgment contradicts their noble self-image. It is humiliating to be judged in the court of international public opinion for events that occurred before the Republic of Turkey was even born. In addition, the government of Turkey fears that the campaign is laying the legal groundwork for reparations or territorial claims. Ankara also worries that Armenia wants to repossess ancestral homelands, such as Mount Ararat. Turkish nationalists still believe the country is surrounded by hostile powers seeking to destroy it.

Kocharian addressed these concerns during an interview with Turkey's leading journalist, Mehmet Ali Birand. After I confirmed arrangements for the meeting, Birand flew with his CNN/Turk camera crew to Yerevan in an old Armenian Airlines Tupelov propeller plane. The interview was worth the trip. Kocharian told Birand, "I know in Turkey some people think if the genocide were recognized Armenia would present Turkey with territorial claims. [However], genocide recognition will not lead to legal consequences or territorial claims."[16] Kocharian's assurance helped mollify concerns about Armenia's intentions. It also helped create a conducive atmosphere for the next phase of Track Two.

Notes

1. Correspondence to members of the U.S. Congress, October 12, 2000.
2. Statement by Ambassador Robert Pearson, October 5, 2000.

3. Paul Wolfowitz, 2002 Turgut Ozal Memorial Lecture, Washington Institute on Near East Policy.
4. *Turkish Daily News,* July 21, 2001.
5. Interview with the author, August 6, 2003.
6. Interview with the author, August 5, 2003.
7. Ibid.
8. Mathew Berkowitz, "The Dark World of the Armenians," *The Jerusalem Post,* September 22, 2003.
9. *The Armenian Genocide: News Accounts from the American Press 1915–22,* edited by Richard D. Kloian, Armenian Genocide Resource Center of Northern California, 2000.
10. Samantha Power, "A Problem from Hell: America and the Age of Genocide," HarperCollins Publishers, 2003.
11. Interview with President Robert Kocharian by Mehmet Ali Birand, February 23, 2001.
12. *Turkish Daily News,* July 12, 2001.
13. Remarks by Foreign Minister Vartan Oskanian, TESEV, Istanbul, June 26, 2002.
14. Gunduz Aktan, "And Now France," *Turkish Daily News,* November 1, 2000.
15. Memo from PDAS/ECA Helena Finn, December 15, 2000.
16. Interview with President Robert Kocharian by Mehmet Ali Birand, February 23, 2001.

4

EMPATHY

Whereas the June 2000 meeting in Vienna was a classic Track Two exercise that included academics and civil society representatives, the follow-up meeting was much more politically charged. Having tacitly endorsed the truth and reconciliation process, the Turkish and Armenian governments had a keen interest in the outcome. Both sent "unofficial" representatives to keep an eye on the discussions.

The Armenian delegation included David Hovhanissian, a trusted confidant of Armenia's foreign minister. Formerly Armenia's ambassador to Syria, David had been appointed "minister at-large" for regional issues. He is also a professor at Yerevan State University where he is beloved as a brilliant academician and expert in Koranic studies. David is the strong-silent type, who listens to jazz and often speaks fondly of his grandson. He attended the meeting in his private capacity.

Van Krikorian and David were joined by Alex Arzoumanian, Armenia's former foreign minister and ambassador to the United Nations. During the administration of Levon Ter-Petrossian, Alex had tried unsuccessfully to establish diplomatic relations with Turkey. Though Alex's wife is from Philadelphia, the Arzoumanians elected to raise their family in Yerevan. Alex is deeply concerned about the effect of Turkey's blockade on Armenia's prospects.

Ozdem Sanberk was on the Turkish side. As undersecretary of state, Ozdem's responsibilities included bilateral relations between Turkey and Azerbaijan. He played a pivotal role during the coup of 1995. His participation ensured that Baku's interest would be looked after. Ozdem was joined by Gunduz Aktan. Despite their status as "former officials," both Ozdem and Gunduz maintain close contact with the foreign ministry.

Gunduz is especially wired with state structures, including representatives of the National Security Council.

We went to a Mozart concert at a small theater in the old city. I hoped the performance would have a calming effect on the group. The Armenians were worried about Gunduz. To them, he is the ultimate "denier." Gunduz had confirmed his ultranationalist reputation during his combative congressional testimony on H.R. 596.

The meeting was businesslike. Armenian participants emphasized the need for an open discussion about the Armenian genocide. The Turks said they were prepared to discuss any topic. Whenever we reached a decision point, Gunduz and Ozdem would go outside to use their cell phones. It seemed as though they were acting on instructions from the Turkish government.

Over two days of intense discussion, we devised a plan to set up some sort of commission with working groups on historical, psychological, and legal matters. We discussed focusing the history group's work on different periods: the rise of nationalism (1878–85); the reign of Sultan Abdul Hamid (1886–96); events during the late nineteenth and early twentieth centuries (1896–1922); and contemporary relations (1965 and 1972–present).[1] Spanning a century of Turkish-Armenian relations would provide historical context by including the Armenian rebellion, the Armenian genocide, and Armenian terrorist activities during the 1970s and 1980s.

Since the Turks were wary of locking in an agenda or timetable, we agreed on "the importance of building confidence through an incremental approach and a flexible work plan." We also agreed that "All matters concerning the Reconciliation Commission will be closely held by the participants and will not be disclosed to the public."[2] Participants wanted to prepare the ground by nurturing supporters and explaining the initiative to potential detractors.

* * *

A larger group met a month later in Vienna. The Turkish side was joined by Ilter Turkmen, who served as foreign minister from 1980 to 1983 and later as UN undersecretary-general. Ilter recounted his first visit to Armenia. In 1941, Ilter was on holiday visiting his father, the military attaché at the Turkish embassy in Moscow. When the German Luftwaffe started bombing, he and other family dependents were bundled onto a Soviet train and rushed out of the city. After seventeen days, the group entered Armenia; passed through Gyumri; and finally crossed the border into Turkey at Kars. Ilter was not aware of problems between Turks and Armenians until ASALA started assassinating Turkish diplomats. Ilter recounted how "As foreign minister, I was constantly going to the funerals. I had a file of all the eulogies I gave honoring Turkey's best diplomats."[3] Despite this experience, Ilter emerged as one of TARC's key members. Ilter is a wise man whose gentlemanly demeanor and steady hand were invaluable. When TARC almost collapsed the following year, Ilter and Van met discreetly on numerous occasions to keep the process going.

Ustun Erguder is a balanced and urbane man who carries himself with great dignity. Introducing himself in Vienna, Ustun described his first encounter with the Armenian issue. "As a graduate student at Manchester University, I would spend hours at the library. One day I came across a stack of independent sources describing the final years of the Ottoman Empire. It was a big discovery."[4] Ustun went on to a distinguished career in academia. After retiring as rector of Bogazici University, he founded the Istanbul Policy Center at Sabanci University. As the one true civil society representative among TARC's Turkish members, Ustun would emerge as a heroic champion of reconciliation. I was introduced to Ustun and Ilter by Helena Finn.

Sadi Erguvenc is a well-respected retired three-star general who was commander at Incirlik Air Force Base during the Gulf War. Though Sadi is by nature moderate, he has close connections to Turkey's security establishment and follows the state line. After retiring from active duty, Sadi assumed a position at the all-powerful National Security Council Secretariat. He is a frequent participant at international conferences. Sitting handsomely in the front row, Sadi puts a smiling face on Turkey's often-contentious neighborly relations.

Gunduz invited Vamik Volkan, a professor of psychiatry from the University of Virginia at Charlottesville. Vamik has many accomplishments as a scholar and Track Two practitioner. However, his approach did not resonate with participants who felt as though they were being psychoanalyzed. As a result, Vamik only participated in a few of the meetings. Issues about the psychology of trauma and identity would recur in our discussions. His departure was a loss.

Herbert C. Kelman, a Harvard University professor and godfather of multitrack diplomacy, disputes whether TARC was really Track Two as some members were acting on instructions from their governments.[5] I selected the Turkish TARC members precisely because of their ties to the government of Turkey. I envisioned their connection to the bureaucracy as an asset. Not only are they familiar with the attitudes of Turkish officials we were looking to influence, their reputation as defenders of the state was needed to neutralize critics of TARC in Ankara.

Turkey operates under a siege mentality with many Turks believing that the world is against them. They point to the 1920 Treaty of Sèvres as evidence of an international conspiracy to break up the country. After

World War I, the Allies attempted to impose Sèvres on the Ottoman Empire. Instead Ataturk defeated the Allies at Gallipoli, won the War of Independence, and created a modern, secular republic along European lines. Many Turks believe that the Treaty of Sèvres was an attempt by Great Powers to carve up spheres of influence and constrain Turkey's ambitions. The "Sèvres syndrome" is based on the belief that outside powers would like to weaken and divide Turkey. Ilter insists that "Sèvres lived as a legend which was recently revived by nationalists."[6] Somehow we lost the self-confidence that Ataturk had inspired."[7]

TARC discussed the opaque process of decision-making in Turkey. The so-called deep state includes the military, intelligence, and the bureaucracy. It arose as a response to weak governments unable to control events in the country. The deep state exercises its extraordinary power to defend against threats, real or imagined. It is a clandestine operation with no legal mandate or authorization from the parliament. It influences social and political institutions shaping society in service of the status quo. Its web of cadres, institutions, rules, and regulations is omnipotent and omnipresent.

As the champion of Turkey's sovereignty, the deep state opposes efforts to join the European Union. It is wary of civilian control over the military and opposes transparency of its expenditures. The deep state obstructs progress on Cyprus, discussion about Armenia, and improvements in Kurdish human rights. Perpetuating these problems allows it to preserve a privileged position. Lacking threats, Kemalist hawks could not justify 750,000 troops under arms.

The deep state's goal to protect the nation has been corrupted by a lack of transparency. Civil servants are seduced by its absolute power. Even Turkey's business elite, who have earned a reputation for taking on the government, almost never confront the deep state. They are beholden for financing from state-owned banks. They profit from state contracts and need state-issued licenses. Large corporate holding companies also own all the media outlets, which support the state's interest. Turkey's giant patronage system is controlled by a privileged group bent on retaining power.*

Though it was essential to gain credibility by including retired diplomats, Ustun would later lament that TARC was "colonized by [officials]. We needed an inroad into the foreign ministry, but we should not have let them dominate it."[8]

I kept pressing Van to enlarge the group of Armenians, but only one new Armenian joined TARC. Andranik Migranian is experienced, tough, and articulate. He served as senior foreign policy advisor to Boris Yeltsin and is a leader of the Armenian Community in Russia and a professor at

---

*Reforms linked to Turkey's EU candidacy are marginalizing the deep state.

Moscow State University. To TARC's Armenian members, Andranik played the same role as Gunduz. He is an aggressive proponent of Armenian national interests who is always on the offensive.

* * *

We were all impatient during the opening night's performance of Austrian chamber music. The stiff wooden chairs were uncomfortable. The concert chamber was hot and the performance was lackluster. Everyone was keen to get to work.

The next morning, we launched into a structured discussion on historical, psychological, and legal issues affecting the commission's activities. David started off by asking, "Who are we?" Addressing the burden of history, he explained how the Armenian genocide had galvanized the formation of a collective identity for Armenians worldwide. Though eighty-five years have passed, Armenians are still angered over past losses. To this day, they feel anxiety about their safety and future security. In response to collective pain and suffering, Armenians find solace in their family and Church, which enable connection to the wider identity group. Turkey's denial of the genocide affects the collective self-esteem of Armenians. The refusal of most Turks to acknowledge their suffering contributes to an overwhelming sense of injustice—and rage.

I witnessed the effect of denial on Armenians when, a few months later, TARC interviewed retired Turkish ambassadors Omer Lutem and Mumtaz Soysal. When the Armenians tried to explain the grief of being driven from their homes, Lutem retorted, "Turkish books do not show any Armenian presence before the Turks. Anatolia was never an Armenian homeland. You were just visitors." When Alex pointed out that they were in Anatolia long enough to build more than four thousand churches, Soysal added, "We tried to destroy them all, but there were just too many." Then Lutem threatened, "If Armenians insist on genocide, Turkey will inflict hurt on Armenia. Is that what you want?" We wondered if Lutem and Soysal were really that hateful. Were their remarks intended to humiliate or were they designed to provoke a confrontation?[9]

Though Lutem and Soysal are extreme examples, even passive denial stirs a desire for revenge. Armenians want justice for the wrongs committed against them. Justice holds individuals accountable for their crimes. It also involves public acknowledgment, which can lead to resolution and closure. In addition, justice means the dismantling of institutions that were instruments of oppression. The administration of justice helps deter future abuses and violations.[10]

The need for justice poses a problem for Armenians. The Ottoman Empire no longer exists and individuals who committed crimes have been dead for years. Since Turkey refuses to acknowledge the genocide,

Armenians believe that the only recourse is to seek recognition from foreign governments and in the court of worldwide public opinion. Without acknowledgment, their mourning is incomplete and Armenians are compelled to remember what was lost.

Dr. Anie Kalayjian believes that the explicit expression of remorse has enormous healing value, but the victim must not be passive in pursuing it. She writes, "Forgiving the perpetrator breaks the cycle of anger, accusation and recrimination. Many Armenians confuse forgiveness with forgetting."[11] The cycle of hatred can also be broken when the victim acknowledges how their actions may have contributed to their victimization. In 1949 Chojiro Kuriyama, a member of the Japanese Diet, apologized for Japan's role in events leading up to the bombing of Hiroshima and Nagasaki. "It is our sincere regret that Japan has broken an almost century old friendship between our countries."[12] In a similar vein, Franco-German friendship would not have been possible absent Germany's recognition of its aggression and regret for the Holocaust.

Appreciating the context of events must not be used, however, to justify moral equivalency. For example, Armenians reacted with scorn when Turkey's State Archives released documents refuting the genocide of Armenians by claiming that it was actually Armenians who committed systematic massacres. Some Turks insist that Armenians brought massacres on themselves by betraying the Ottoman Empire. Instead of mutual understanding, such assertions further polarize positions and entrench antagonistic views.[13]

David explained that genocide recognition is essential for reconciliation. "I believe the future holds a lot of opportunities for Armenians and Turks," added Andranik. "We have shared a very important common history. It would be good to focus on future opportunities for cooperation—opening up borders, economic relations, and cultural activities. Once you get this rolling, then you can look at history in a more detached manner."[14] Ustun believes that the key to reconciliation is "opening the borders, discussing diplomatic relations and putting the genocide in the freezer for a while."[15] However, David cautions that "Looking ahead does not preclude remembering the past."[16]

"We Turks do not look to our past," explained Gunduz. "We never heard of our sufferings. Instead we look to the future. The Republic was formed upon the amnesia of this pain."[17] Gunduz was referring to the final years of the Ottoman Empire. From the Adriatic to the Caspian, Ottoman territories were lost as the empire collapsed. "Millions were killed or driven from their homes. This was not simply the case of losing land. Millions of people were brutally murdered, maimed and exiled. All the people of Anatolia took part in the final score-settling. A joint history of togetherness was destroyed."[18]

Turks prefer to focus on past glories. A selective reading of history highlights the achievements of sultans and their heroic feats in battle. Educated Turks know about Sultan Selim I who conquered North Africa. In 1517, Selim took the Prophet Mohammed's holy relics from Cairo to Constantinople. From then on, the Ottoman Sultans were also Caliphs— representatives of the Prophet and leaders of a community of believers in Sunni Islam. Selim's son, Suleiman the Magnificent, is also celebrated. He advanced to the gates of Vienna and ruled half of Europe. Ottoman administration at the time was benign and enlightened. As long as they were obedient and paid taxes on time, conquered peoples were allowed to keep their leadership and maintain communal traditions. Though minorities were subordinate to local lords ("Beys") and regional commanders ("Pashas"), the "Millet system" permitted religious communities to administer their own affairs, allowing religious groups to flourish.

In response to efforts by European powers to diminish the country, Ataturk emphasized the inviolability of Turkey's borders. Turks never dwell on their defeats, pretending failures never happened. For example, there are no archives recounting the tragedies that occurred at the end of the Ottoman Empire. Records have been sanitized. The Republic of Turkey is a country with selective memory.

A discussion ensued on the psychodynamics of political conflict. Vamik suggested that the most difficult conflicts are those where both sides have suffered traumatic loss. There are many people in Turkey today whose ancestors were victims of pogroms in the Balkans, Caucasus, and territories on the Black Sea. He explained that Turks are tired of being accused. They too experienced losses, and need empathy for their suffering. Reconciliation can never be achieved until both sides overcome resistance to hearing one another and develop empathy for their shared tragedies. Kelman explains, "Track Two participants speak to be understood and listen to understand."[19]

As a Turkish Cypriot, Vamik has personal experience with ethnic conflict and the tragedy of communal violence. He described his first contact with an Armenian. Growing up, Vamik loved to play the violin. He was very fond of his Armenian music teacher. Vamik's early associations with Armenians were influenced by his appreciation for the violin and affection for his teacher. Tears welled up in his eyes as he talked about her.

Vamik explained his work on the psychodynamics of conflict between Greek and Turkish Cypriots. According to Vamik, the root cause of contemporary conflict is the psychological distress felt by traumatized populations. The symptoms of post-traumatic stress disorder are loss of basic trust, difficulty in mourning, and a sense of helplessness and humiliation passed from generation to generation. Both Greek and Turkish Cypriot historians have large libraries justifying their views on the division of

Cyprus. We laughed when Vamik said that historians can never agree on anything.

Vamik prefers to work with civil society representatives. He believes that senior political leaders are poor candidates for psychodynamic work. They are deeply invested in their public image and, as politicians, have limited room to maneuver outside the requirements of their constituencies. Moreover, politicians may seek political gain by stirring feelings of anger associated with unfulfilled justice. They do this by highlighting a "chosen trauma." For example, Slobodan Milosevic awakened virulent Serbian nationalism by invoking a memory of betrayal, sacrifice, and death. He disinterred the bones of Prince Lazar, Serbia's great warrior who perished during the Battle of Kosovo in 1389, and displayed them across the country as a reminder to Serbs of their unrequited struggle against the Muslim Turks.

"Chosen trauma" allows the victim to become intensely absorbed by their own losses. Their preoccupation makes it hard to appreciate that the victimizers may also have been victims at some point. Vamik believes it is impossible to achieve reconciliation without addressing the psychological needs of both the victim and victimizer. Gunduz explained, "There is no way a regime that did not teach its own children the anguish of their past could feel the anguish of another."[20]

* * *

Gunduz and Andranik sat together during lunch in the garden of the Diplomatic Academy. Both are doggedly determined proponents of their respective nationalist views. It seemed as though our morning discussion had an effect. They strolled together, sipping coffee, while Gunduz puffed his cigar. Their capacity for constructive interaction would be severely tested that afternoon.

After lunch, Gunduz presented a paper on the evolution of international humanitarian law, culminating in the Nuremberg trials and adoption of the United Nations Convention on the Prevention and Punishment for Crimes of Genocide (December 9, 1948). He focused extensively on the definition of genocide in the convention. Gunduz maintained that Armenians were not killed because they were an ethnic, racial, or religious group, as such. They were expelled for rebelling against the Ottoman Empire. The decision to deport the Armenians was not based on who they were, but on what they did. He asserted, "Given the fact that the Armenians in the Ottoman Empire made up a political group fighting for national independence, crimes against them do not constitute genocide. There was no racial hatred towards the Armenians in Ottoman Turkey."[21] In addition, Gunduz argued that the Genocide Convention is not applicable to events in the early twentieth century because international agreements are not applied retroactively. To resolve this issue once and for all, he proposed that the Republics of Turkey and Armenia submit their cases for arbitration by the International Court of Justice in The Hague.

The Armenians were incensed. Van tried to calm tensions by talking about the treaty's intent, but the discussion quickly degenerated into squabbling, accusations, and finger pointing. Fortunately, an attendant from the Diplomatic Academy knocked on the door and wheeled a tray of coffee and pastries into the room. Our coffee break came not a moment too soon.

I decided it would not be productive to continue talking about legal issues. The morning's goodwill had dissipated, and the process might derail if acrimonious discussions were allowed to continue. Instead I asked the group to consider an implementing structure for future activities. We had already agreed on a format and work plan at our last meeting. I thought to get back on track by focusing on areas of previous agreement.

Gunduz was still agitated from the earlier discussion. I had seen him and Vamik caucusing during the break. Vamik weighed in to support Gunduz's concerns. He urged us to be patient. Before rushing forward with reconciliation projects, Vamik argued that the core group must undergo its own transformation. He suggested we take more time to get to know one another, appreciate differences, and develop empathy. Establishing trust could take years, he added.

Without relenting, Gunduz stayed on the offensive. He insisted that progress was impossible unless the Armenians abandoned their campaign for international genocide recognition. He warned against efforts by the Armenian Diaspora to organize a new genocide resolution in the U.S. Congress. "Passage of another resolution will generate great hostility towards Armenia," he threatened.[22]

The Armenians felt that Gunduz and Vamik were just stonewalling. Everyone else had been getting along just fine, until Gunduz started to dominate the discussion. The meeting was on the verge of collapse. I announced a break and took Gunduz for a walk in the garden.

I told him that we were at a dead end. It was my intention to reconvene the group and announce that the meeting was adjourned. Moreover, there would be no more meetings in the future. I told Gunduz that he had poisoned the well, and that I would make sure it was known in both Washington and Ankara that he had sabotaged the initiative. Gunduz protested; I told him that the only way to save the process would be to make clear his support for an organization facilitating collaborative activities. Like some TARC members, I too was using my government connections to compel progress.

Our colleagues were nervously waiting when we reentered the room. Taking the floor, Gunduz carefully chose his words in reaffirming the importance of reconciliation and recommitting his support. There was a collective sigh of relief. The reconciliation commission had tottered on the edge of collapse. We had dodged a bullet. Vamik expressed the sentiments of the group by acknowledging our near miss and offering his respect to everyone. I picked up on Vamik's positive contribution by asking participants to describe their personal hopes.

Andranik told a story about his family from Mush, an ancient Armenian town in central Anatolia. He described how his grandparents and their neighbors were rounded up and deported. He always dreamed of going back to his family's ancestral lands and visiting the old homestead. He hoped to honor their memory by finding Turks who would take moral responsibility for their tragedy.

Ozdem responded by a telling a family story of his own. His grandparents came from a village in Macedonia. When the Ottoman Empire collapsed, they were forced to abandon their property and flee penniless from the Balkans. They were lucky to escape. Hundreds of thousands of Muslims in Macedonia were brutally slaughtered by vengeful Serbs and Bulgarians. Ozdem reminded Andranik that both families had suffered a similar fate and that, as their descendants, they had a responsibility to right the wrongs of the past.

Gunduz interjected, "Do you know how we feel when you try to embarrass us by introducing resolutions in parliaments around the world? Our feelings are hurt." "Your feelings are hurt. How do you think we feel?" responded Alex. "We were the ones who were genocided."[23]

Van brought the group back to business by emphasizing next steps. He proposed that we institutionalize our work by establishing the commission. We agreed that historical, legal, and psychological experts could advise us, but that the core group would take the lead in identifying policy options. Ilter said, "Turkey does not have courageous politicians. We can't leave the job to them. They are not up to it. We should focus on shaping public opinion."[24]

For the first time, Turks and Armenians had really listened to one another. Though they may have snickered at Vamik's plea for empathy, they had indeed passed a threshold. Ozdem wrote, "It was a very useful meeting, but most of all the atmosphere of friendship which prevailed among us was the most important reward we can ever obtain."[25]

My chairman's statement indicated that "We had an emotional discussion about personal experiences [that] enhanced mutual understanding and strengthened common purpose."[26] Real friendship, however, takes time to cultivate. Despite progress, we needed much more time together. Given the personalities of some members, I wondered if TARC could cohere as a group.

The Armenians were focused on milestones. Instead of lingering over the process of team building, we agreed to adopt terms of reference at our next meeting and publicly announce the Turkish-Armenian Reconciliation Commission (TARC). To move discussions along, I was asked to draft TARC's founding charter.

Notes

1. Chairman's Statement, March 20, 2001.
2. Ibid.
3. Interview with the author, January 17, 2004.
4. Interview with the author, January 15, 2004.
5. Interview with the author, January 9, 2004.
6. Interview with the author, August 6, 2003.
7. Interview with the author, January 17, 2004.
8. Interview with the author, August 6, 2003.
9. Meeting notes, September 24, 2001.
10. Joseph V. Montville, "Justice and the Burdens of History," published in *Reconciliation, Coexistence and Justice in Interethnic Conflict,* edited by Mohammed Abu Nimer, Lexington Books, 2001.
11. Anie Kalayjian, "Forgiveness and Transcendence," published in *Clio's Psyche,* December 1999.
12. Joseph V. Montville, "The Greening of Diplomacy," *Journal of the American Psychoanalytic Association,* Vol. 31, No. 2.
13. Announcement by Turkey's State Archives Directorate General, April 22, 2003.
14. *Radio Free Europe,* January 13, 2002.
15. Interview with the author, August 6, 2003.
16. Meeting notes, May 30, 2001.
17. Gunduz Aktan, "The Pot Calling the Kettle Black," *Turkish Daily News,* October 20, 2001.
18. Ibid.
19. Interview with the author, January 9, 2004.
20. Aktan, "The Pot Calling the Kettle Black."
21. Meeting notes, April 30, 2001.
22. Ibid.
23. Ibid.
24. Ibid.
25. E-mail from Sanberk to Krikorian, May 1, 2001.
26. Chairman's Statement, April 30, 2001.

5

A Historic Step

I had been keeping Doug Frantz, the *New York Times* correspondent in Istanbul, informed of efforts to set up the reconciliation commission. He traveled to Armenian ancestral homelands in eastern Turkey and was interested in writing about TARC. I told him TARC would finalize plans at its meeting on July 9, 2001. Just in case something went wrong, Frantz agreed to hold the story until I called him to confirm that the terms of reference had been formally adopted and that TARC members had agreed to go public.[1]

At the meeting, I made clear to TARC members that there was no going back once we announced the initiative. There had never been a comparable effort and, if we failed, there might not be another for many years to come. Cognizant of TARC's importance, they agreed to go forward.

While some Track Two efforts adopt strict rules of confidentiality, TARC knew that information about its work would leak out. Therefore, it decided to adopt a proactive media strategy shaping public discourse to secure support. By releasing information about TARC in the *New York Times,* we hoped that Frantz's story would serve as the reference point for the international media, as well as Turkish and Armenian journalists. I arranged for Frantz to interview Elie Wiesel, whose moral authority would enhance TARC's credibility.

I reentered the conference room at the Centre for Humanitarian Dialogue on Lake Geneva to find TARC's Turkish members talking feverishly on their cell phones. Some were also on the computer sending electronic copies of TARC's charter to well-placed Turkish media. More than an hour passed while the Turks worked the phones. Ilter Turkmen and Gunduz Aktan have regular columns in leading Turkish papers and agreed to write about the initiative.

In contrast, the Armenians were nonchalant. Van Krikorian had already briefed leading Armenian political, religious, and civic leaders. He was confident that the first structured dialogue between Turks and Armenians would be warmly welcomed by some, opposed by others, but was the right course to follow. David Hovhanissian called Vartan Oskanian to confirm that an agreement had been reached and that the announcement would appear in tomorrow's *New York Times.* Oskanian's response was surprising. He instructed David to say that he had left the foreign ministry and was participating in his private capacity. At the same time, he told David that he was expected in his office at the ministry on Monday morning.

David was visibly shaken when he returned to the meeting. I had met with Oskanian on several occasions to brief him. At every turn, he endorsed the initiative. Robert Kocharian also directly communicated his support for TARC. Though Kocharian had been briefed personally and knew when TARC would go public, I was concerned that Oskanian's reaction meant that the support of Armenian leaders might not be so steadfast after all.

TARC's Armenian members kept their concerns to themselves. When TARC reconvened that afternoon, we discussed issues affecting contact between Turkish and Armenian civil society. The recent pilgrimage of Armenians to Turkey was instructive of both the opportunities and pitfalls to cooperation.

Two dozen Armenians had just toured Armenian historical and sacred sites in Turkey. Their pilgrimage coincided with the 1,700-year anniversary of Christianity in Armenia. "The group had no problems with Turkish authorities and even received the 'royal treatment' in Kars where the Mayor and other city officials welcomed them."[2] Despite feelings of amity, the trip was not a complete success. Ankara had assured the Turkish-Armenian Business Development Council that the group would be allowed to visit the ancient Armenian city of Ani, and then cross the border into Armenia. They were informed at the last moment that permission had been revoked.

TARC was much more focused on policy initiatives than "feel-good" citizen exchanges. While TARC's Armenian members recognized the importance of cultural projects, they focused on opening Turkey's border and establishing diplomatic relations. They had limited patience for small steps or confidence building. Andranik Migranian would raise the bar even higher by insisting that TARC address the genocide issue. "Culture is nice but we need to come to an understanding on the genocide and other issues that divide us." If not, he warned, "We will continue to raise genocide in parliaments around the world."[3]

The Turks stiffened. They had no appetite for discussing the genocide, nor did they take kindly to Andranik's threat. Vamik Volkan responded, "Okay, you have us by the balls, and we have you by the balls. Do pressure tactics help us?" Echoing his concern, Gunduz objected to plans by the Armenian-American community to build an Armenian Genocide Museum in Washington, D.C. Van described his hope that the museum would include an exhibit on reconciliation. Not only would it tell the story of righteous Turks who saved Armenians, it might also highlight TARC's role in rebuilding relations between the two communities. "You want our empathy, but you have no empathy for us," Gunduz protested.[4]

Throwing fuel on the fire, Ozdem Sanberk asked how TARC would handle the "occupied territories" that had been forcefully seized by ethnic Armenians in Azerbaijan. Would TARC call for the return of Azeris displaced from their homes? Ozdem underscored the deep historical and cultural ties between Turks and Azeris. Since Azerbaijan's independence, Ankara linked normalization of relations with Armenia to a settlement of the dispute over Nagorno-Karabakh. Alex Arzoumanian objected. "We should not discuss Nagorno-Karabakh. It is a conflict with a third country that has nothing to do with Turkey and Armenia."[5]

Referring to TARC's handling of the genocide, Ilter asked, "Does this mean we cannot move forward until the big issue is resolved?" Ilter was always a voice of reason. No matter how heated the discussion, he was always elegant and respectful. Ilter urged TARC to focus on small steps. Instead of arguing about the most difficult issues, he encouraged specific projects demonstrating the practical value of cooperation. Vamik agreed that it was premature to tackle the genocide issue. First TARC should strengthen the bonds between its founding members.

Despite their agreement to go forward, it was apparent that the Turks and Armenians had fundamentally different expectations of TARC. The Armenians saw TARC as a vehicle for approaching Turkish elites and initiating a dialogue about the genocide. Even if Turks are sympathetic to the suffering of Armenians, they were not prepared to have TARC acknowledge the genocide. Gunduz maintained, "None of the Turkish participants considered the events of 1915–16 as genocide. Our position was explained to the other side many times in our heated talks."[6]

TARC agreed to try to build a better understanding of respective positions. Though the hard-line approach of some members raised doubts about the usefulness of their participation, we were convinced that dialogue would make it possible for Turks to develop an increased appreciation for the suffering of Armenians. In turn, Armenians would also become more empathic of the tragedy that befell many Turks at the end of the Ottoman Empire. The goal of fostering human relations and building mutual understanding might have been more realizable with different participants. By including individuals closely linked to the establishment in their countries, TARC traded amity for the hope of substantive progress. The trade-off might have been worth it had TARC, in fact, achieved a major policy breakthrough.

* * *

To kick-start discussion on civil society activities, Ozdem presented some project proposals prepared by the Turkish Economic and Social Studies Foundation (TESEV). The foundation was established by members of the business community and had a liberal reputation. Ozdem proposed that his think tank work with an Armenian counterpart to conduct sociological research on Armenian attitudes toward Turks and Turkish attitudes toward Armenians. Gunduz abruptly interrupted Ozdem's presentation on survey methodology, saying that he "could never agree to this project." The Turks started arguing amongst themselves. As their discussion became more heated, they switched from English to Turkish.

Strong disagreements between the Turkish and Armenian members of TARC were expected. Deep division among the Turks was not. Not only were there differences in approach, the Turks were divided by temperament as well. Gunduz was the feistiest. Tensions lingered between Ilter and Gunduz from their clashes when Ilter was foreign minister. Like Gunduz, Ozdem was Ilter's subordinate. However, Ozdem showed deference to his former boss. Ustun complained that some of TARC's members acted more like officials than private citizens. Instead of behaving like civil society and exploring ideas without constraint, they undermined the Track Two process by reverting to official positions.

Gunduz asked for a break so that the Turks could discuss matters. After they had some time to themselves, I pulled Gunduz aside to explore his concerns. When the meeting was called to order, we agreed that it was too early to develop joint projects and the dossier of project proposals was set aside. It would also be inappropriate to endorse other activities. TARC should try to stay informed of Turkish-Armenian projects, but it should not try to control them. Instead TARC should focus on its own work.

We agreed that TARC should listen to others and develop strategies accordingly. At our next meeting in Istanbul, we would invite different civil society representatives to advise TARC on how it could most effectively advance the goal of reconciliation. To get a range of views, we would interview "liberal" intellectuals as well as ultranationalists.

TARC had avoided disputes by deferring critical decisions on strategy, priorities, and approach. It decided to focus on the easiest issues first in order to create an atmosphere conducive to tackling more intractable problems. This understanding worked well when we were together. But it was much more difficult under the glare of public scrutiny.

Differences were exposed when TARC met with members of the international press later that afternoon. Though TARC had given the *New York Times* an exclusive, we also wanted the wire services to write about the initiative. Their reports would be picked up worldwide as an announcement of TARC's establishment. We discussed procedures for the press conference, and agreed that Ilter would speak on behalf of the group. The Turks asked me to maintain a low profile. They did not want it to look as though the State Department imposed TARC on them.

Ilter issued an opening statement to correspondents from the Associated Press, Agence France Press, and Reuters. Their first question concerned how TARC would deal with the genocide issue. Ilter tried to answer for the group; Van amplified on his remarks; Gunduz jumped in. Ever tactful, Ilter blandished, "It seems we get along much better when the media is not present."[7]

* * *

Problems with media relations would constantly plague TARC. It would adopt principles for interacting with the press only to have them ignored. In retrospect, TARC failed to implement an effective media relations plan. It also jumped the gun by disclosing its activities before arriving at a common message or achieving coherence as a group. Ustun Erguder would later reflect, "I will never forget when the press walked into the room in Geneva. The Armenians started talking, not to us, but to their constituency."[8]

Frantz's story appeared in the *New York Times* on July 10, 2001. He described TARC's terms of reference. Regarding the genocide, he quoted Ilter: "The commission will not determine the validity of either position. Instead, it will explore ways to bridge the gap." Frantz wrote, "The participants, including some former officials, have been meeting discreetly for months. The Turkish and Armenian governments are not involved, but participants said both had given tacit approval. The State Department supported the initiative."[9]

U.S. government officials and other interested parties issued statements of support. Marc Grossman wrote, "The civil society contacts that have taken place are encouraging, and we believe that both Turkey and Armenia are intent on making progress. We continue to have confidence that civil society and government to government dialogue will best enable Armenia and Turkey to move beyond their painful past toward a more peaceful future. This administration believes a people-to-people initiative such as the Reconciliation Commission is a big step forward."[10]

TARC was also endorsed by Frank Pallone (D-NJ) and Joe Knollenberg (R-MI), cochairmen of the Congressional Caucus on Armenian Issues.

"We welcome news that the Commission has been established. We believe this high level effort is a positive step forward and will benefit the people of both nations. We urge all Armenian-Americans to support this opportunity."[11]

Ambassador Edward Djerejian, the former Assistant Secretary of State for Near Eastern Affairs and a respected confidant of the Bush administration, wrote, "The creation of a private group, the Turkish-Armenian Reconciliation Commission is a welcome and positive development."[12] His endorsement was echoed by Harry Gilmore, the former U.S. ambassador to Armenia. "The Commission is a major breakthrough in Turkish-Armenian relations, which would do much to enhance mutual understanding."[13]

TARC was welcomed in Europe. The European parliament's 2001 report on Turkey's progress toward accession indicated that the parliament "supports the civil initiative launched by a group of former diplomats and academics from Turkey and Armenia, the aim of which is to arrive at a common understanding of the past; [and] hopes that this initiative will contribute towards the normalization of relations between the two communities concerned." The international media also responded favorably. A *Washington Times* editorial said, "TARC is a step in the right direction—and a reflection of Turkey's and Armenia's maturity and goodwill."[14] The *Toronto Globe and Mail* wrote, "TARC is "praiseworthy. Just as Turkey knows the world is changing, so it must change."[15]

The Turkish press was also enthusiastic. They were pleased that Armenians were ready to reconcile and hoped that TARC might marginalize Armenian extremists. Turkish TARC members were respected and, because of their state connections, the media anticipated they would not deviate from Ankara's official position.

Ilter was surrounded by journalists when he got off the plane from Geneva in Istanbul. Ilter reflected, "This is not the first time that Turks and Armenians have come together, but it is the first time there has been a structured dialogue."[16] He asserted that TARC would not seek to arrive at a historical judgment, nor did TARC members expect an immediate resolution of problems. "Historical perceptions will not change from one day to another."[17] Ozdem also offered assurances stating that "The intent is not to find out what the truth is, but to open new horizons for the future and enhance mutual understanding."[18] "A Historic Breakthrough," announced the headline of *Milliyet*. Sami Kohen, Turkey's leading columnist, wrote, "We view the creation of the Commission ... as timely and in the right direction."[19]

I was worried about the reaction in Turkey. The topic of Turkish-Armenian relations was virtually ignored in Turkish society. To the extent Armenia is considered, it is with resentment for the assassination of Turkish diplomats by ASALA and anger over the displacement of up to one million Azeris from Nagorno-Karabakh. Though reconciliation is a forward-looking process, I knew it would involve some painful reflection for both sides.

In large part because the Turkish members of TARC worked the press and sent all the right signals, the reaction to TARC in Turkey was mature and level headed. A public opinion survey conducted on August 29, 2001, involved 2,458 Turks: 38.5 percent were in favor of dialogue with Armenians, 36.9 percent were against, and 24.7 percent had no opinion.[20] TARC was welcomed in elite intellectual, business, and NGO circles. This could not have happened without the tacit approval of Turkish officials.

Baku's reaction was far less positive. Murtuz Aleskerov, speaker of the Azerbaijan parliament, was visiting Turkey when news of TARC hit the headlines. He denounced the endeavor, saying, "Turkish businessmen who want to do business with Armenia prior to providing for the territorial integrity of our country are betraying Azerbaijan."[21] Noting that TARC's joint statement made no mention of the Nagorno-Karabakh dispute, Ambassador Lutem warned that Baku would be displeased with any effort failing to first address demands by Azerbaijan.

I was not concerned with the response of Armenians. Van had assured me that key Armenians had privately offered assurances of support. For many Armenians reconciling with Turks was much more controversial than I could have ever imagined.

Notes

1. TURKISH-ARMENIAN RECONCILIATION COMMISSION
   Terms of Reference

   Terms of Reference are agreed to on this 9th day of July 2001 between Armenians and Turks from civil society who, working in an individual capacity, agree to establish the *Reconciliation Commission.*

   The Reconciliation Commission grew out of meetings held at the Diplomatic Academy of Vienna.

   The Reconciliation Commission seeks to promote mutual understanding and good will between Turks and Armenians and to encourage improved relations between Armenia and Turkey.

   The Reconciliation Commission appreciates that there are serious differences between Armenians and Turks, as well as obstacles to normal relations between Armenia and Turkey.

   The Reconciliation Commission hopes, through its efforts, to build on the increasing readiness for reconciliation among Turkish and Armenian civil societies including members of Diaspora communities.

   The Reconciliation Commission supports contact, dialogue and cooperation between Armenian and Turkish civil societies in order to create public awareness about the need for reconciliation and to derive practical benefits.

The Reconciliation Commission will directly undertake activities and catalyze projects by other organizations.

The Reconciliation Commission will develop recommendations to be submitted to concerned governments.

The Reconciliation Commission will support collaborative Track Two activities in the fields of business, tourism, culture, education and research, environment, media, confidence building, and other areas which are to be determined.

The Reconciliation Commission will secure expertise based on project requirements, and may include specialists on historical, psychological and legal matters, as well as other topics.

The Reconciliation Commission will review progress after one year.

2. Bill Broadway, "Armenians' Bittersweet Pilgrimage," *The Washington Post,* June 13, 2001.
3. Meeting notes, July 9, 2001.
4. Ibid.
5. Ibid.
6. *Turkish Daily News,* July 13, 2001.
7. Meeting notes, July 9, 2001.
8. Interview with the author, August 6, 2003.
9. Douglas Frantz, "Unofficial Commission Acts to Ease Turkish-Armenian Enmity," *New York Times,* July 10, 2003.
10. Statement by Marc Grossman, Undersecretary of State for Political Affairs, August 27, 2001.
11. Statement on TARC's establishment issued by Representatives Frank Pallone (D-NJ) and Joe Knollenberg (R-MI), cochairmen of the Congressional Caucus on Armenian Issues, July 10, 2001.
12. Statement on TARC's establishment issued by Ambassador Edward Djerejian, director of the James A. Baker Institute for Public Policy, Rice University, September 13, 2001.
13. Statement on TARC's establishment issued by Harry Gilmore, former U.S. ambassador to Armenia, July 13, 2001.
14. Editorial, *Washington Times,* July 17, 2001.
15. Editorial, *Toronto Globe and Mail,* July 12, 2001.
16. "A Historic Step for Turks and Armenians," *Turkish Daily News,* July 12, 2001.
17. "New Commission Set Up to Promote Turkish-Armenian Relations," *Agence France Press,* July 11, 2001.
18. "TARC Formed," *Armenia Report,* July 16, 2001.
19. Sami Kohen, *Milliyet,* July 11, 2001.
20. *Hurriyet,* August 29, 2001.
21. *Turkish Daily News,* July 14, 2001.

6

STORM OF CONTROVERSY

Van Krikorian is a battle-tested champion of the Armenian people. He once described how his Eastern Anatolian ancestors had been murdered and his grandmother, the sole survivor, sold into slavery. She escaped her Turkish captors and, as a refugee, resettled in the United States. Van spoke only Armenian as a child. Like Van, Armenians maintain a strong sense of group identity forged by the suffering of their ancestors.

Except for his aborted business venture in Trabzon, Van had not interacted much with Turks. He worked hard to condemn them, but he had never engaged Turks in a dialogue. His whole life, Van adhered to conventional Armenian political thinking and believed he could pressure Turks into admitting what had happened.

When I met Van Krikorian, he was reevaluating his strategy. He asked, "What is going to help Turkish society change? Is it outside pressure? Those who relied on foreign countries got fine agreements. But the Armenians got nothing and were later abandoned."[1]

Van is driven by a desire to honor the memory of murdered Armenians. Through TARC, he hoped to build a better future. He explained, "At one particularly heated moment, I found myself thinking of my kids. For a long time we have been doing this lobbying work in Washington. When my kids grow up, are they going to be doing the same things, using the same strategies, and hitting the same brick walls? Or will something arise that changes the path they take and the path available to Armenians in Armenia who are being strangled by the blockade?"[2] Van had realized that although "Armenians and Turks continue to be divided, whatever the divisions, they are clearly compounded by the lack of dialogue and direct contact."[3]

Openness to dialogue is the first step toward mutual understanding, which, in turn, is the basis for rapprochement. While some Armenians are sensitive to the feelings of Turks, it is hard for Armenians to appreciate the Turkish view that there was a war, and Armenians lost and paid the price. Others like Sargis Matcharian understand that "There is no issue in the world that has two sides and one face. As long as there are two sides, there are two perspectives, two views of the same issue and two positions."[4]

Van's commitment to TARC was purely tactical. After years of battling the Turks, he realized that "We need to deal with Turkey and with Turks themselves. We need to develop friends and allies who have an interest and see a common benefit to coming to terms with the Armenian Genocide and improving relations with Armenia."[5]

From the outset, Armenian members of TARC saw the commission as a vehicle for accessing Turkey's establishment. They reasoned that the more Turks heard mention of the genocide, the more readily they would accept it as fact. Van explained, "We agreed there can be no true reconciliation until Turks acknowledge the Armenian Genocide. The question is how best to achieve this result. Reconciliation is a process, not an event."[6] Andranik Migranian added, "Ordinary Turks have been told for decades that nothing wrong had happened to the Armenians. The Republic of Turkey cannot declare all of a sudden that something did happen without preparing public opinion."[7]

TARC's announcement received a mostly positive reaction in Armenian society. The Diocesan Council stated, "Armenians and Turks have been separated by a century of bitterness, acrimony and mistrust; and that separation will not be easy to heal. Yet, for the sake of both Armenians and Turks, it must be healed. This new Commission seems to offer real opportunity for improving Armenian-Turkish relations, and we offer our fervent prayers for its success."[8] It was supported by many parties and groups in Armenia, such as the Armenian National Movement, the Union of Socialist Forces, and the Knights of Vartan. In addition, TARC was welcomed by ethnic Armenians in Nagorno-Karabakh. According to "Foreign Minister" Naira Melkumian, "We believe that TARC will be able to find common ground and will try to undo the knots in relations between Armenia and Turkey."[9]

TARC was also supported by a majority of Diaspora Armenians. The editorial page of the widely-read and well-respected *Armenian Reporter* welcomed TARC and consistently supported its reconciliation efforts. The Armenian Assembly of America proclaimed, "After years of talking through intermediaries, the Commission will promote direct dialogue and cooperation to address the issues dividing Armenians and Turks. I firmly believe that it is to the benefit of everyone, particularly those living in the region, to explore any mutually acceptable solution to the problems between Armenia and Turkey."[10]

* * *

Despite the positive response in most Armenian circles, a controversy began swirling around TARC. In both Armenia and the Diaspora, TARC became a bone of contention between parties and groups vying for power and influence. Its critics were vocal—and vicious.

Van recognized that "For some this news was anathema, for others a long overdue step in the right direction and for many more an experiment which requires a wait and see approach."[11] "We shocked a lot of people when we started this. We knew that would happen. We also knew some people would be offended, confused, and jealous for not having been involved."[12]

TARC's detractors accused it of negotiating whether the Armenian genocide actually occurred. They also maintained that TARC's existence was used to deter international criticism of Turkey. In addition, TARC was attacked as a pawn of the U.S. government, and TARC members were labeled traitors. President Kocharian's political opponents used TARC to impugn his leadership. Instead of standing by its commitments, the Kocharian government ran for cover.

Dashnaks questioned the very premise of talking to Turks. They warned that "Any Armenian-Turkish dialogue will yield results only after Turkey accepts the historic fact of the Armenian genocide, something which cannot be the subject of any bargaining."[13] Also demanding that recognition precede dialogue, the Forum of Armenian Associations in Europe called TARC "misconceived and ill-fated."[14] George Aghjayan, a Dashnak mouthpiece, wrote, "Such supposedly noble notions cannot cover the putrid smell of a misguided and ill-conceived scheme. In one sweeping move, the Armenian participants on the commission have given credibility to the Turkish deniers on the commission and legitimacy to their position that Armenians were not subject to genocide. All TARC has advanced is the flawed notion that there are two sides to the events of 1915–1923."[15]

Initially, the Dashnaks agreed to meet and learn more about TARC. But then they refused to discuss it. TARC's most strident critics have no interest in genuine reconciliation. First and foremost, Dashnaks use genocide recognition to solicit money from the Armenian Diaspora. They believe that Turkey must pay for its crimes by returning land and confiscated property. They pursue genocide recognition by foreign governments in part to establish a legal basis for territorial claims and reparations. They also use their campaign to acquire political and economic power. To Dashnaks, TARC was an insidious device undermining their reason for being. Dashnaks have positioned themselves as warriors. If reconciliation occurs, they have no reason to exist. Dashnaks believe that struggle is an end, not a means.

* * *

Some TARC members used the media to address their constituencies. Statements by TARC's Turkish members fueled the belief that Ankara was using TARC to deter genocide recognition by the international community. On a visit to Baku, Ozdem Sanberk announced that "The basic goal of our commission is to impede the initiatives put forth every year in the U.S. Congress and parliaments of Western countries on the genocide issue, which aim to weaken Turkey. The significant matter for us is that the genocide issue is not discussed by the American Congress any more. As long as we continue the dialogue, the issue won't be brought back to the agenda of the Congress."[16]

Ozdem's stated strategy seemed to be working. In 2000, the European Parliament (EP) made Turkey's EU membership conditional on its acceptance of the genocide. The next year, the EP voted down four measures to include genocide in its annual report on Turkey's accession to the EU. Citing TARC as evidence of a softening in Armenian-Turkish relations, EP deputies "consider that the deepening of the dialogue on the question of recognition of the genocide of which the Armenian Community was a victim at the beginning of the 20th century constitutes a significant stage of this normalization."[17] In the period of time immediately following TARC's announcement, the Diaspora failed to gain passage of genocide resolutions in the parliaments of Germany, Switzerland, and Britain. When the German parliament declined to adopt a genocide resolution in September 2001, it cited progress between Turkish and Armenian civil society representatives.

Following Ozdem's statement in Baku, he and Van participated in a panel on Turkish-Armenian relations at the annual conference of the Assembly of Turkish American Associations (ATAA) in Washington, D.C. The Turkish official in the fedora hat was excited. He congratulated me on the arrangement and said, "This is really going to be a historic event."

In his prepared remarks, Ozdem asked, "Why are the Muslim victims of violence in Anatolia and the Balkans so often forgotten, while the Armenian grievances are taken up by the Western world? The non-Muslim refugees from the Ottoman Empire sought to remember, while Muslim refugees wanted mainly to leave their past behind and build a new life. All sides lived through those cruel years and all sides can, hopefully, share each other's pain. Our shared experience could become a bridge between our communities, instead of a gulf that keeps us apart."[18]

The Turkish audience wrote questions on slips of paper that were passed up to me. As moderator, I selected the most reasonable. It was very important that the panel end constructively and without incident. However, Ozdem waited for the final word and, in choreographed fashion, delivered a coup de grace. "The Republic of Turkey will never recognize the Armenian genocide." After the conference, the man in the fedora hat gleefully approached me and said, "I told you this would be historic." When later challenged by Van, Ozdem would apologize, saying, "I am sorry, but I really believe that parliamentary resolutions will kill TARC."[19]

A reporter from the Dashnak newspaper had infiltrated the meeting and Ozdem's pronouncement was headlined the next day. Ozdem had put TARC's Armenian members in an even more defensive position. Responding to accusations that TARC's goal was to derail genocide resolutions, Van retorted, "That's complete nonsense."[20] Alex Arzoumanian maintained, "We are not obstructing international recognition of the genocide. By avoiding talk about it we affirm that it is a historic fact."[21]

Despite their claims, the drumbeat of condemnation grew louder. Parties holding a majority of seats in the Armenian parliament adopted a resolution claiming that TARC intended to remove recognition of the genocide from the international agenda, criticizing TARC's support for Turkey's biased views on Nagorno-Karabakh, and condemning the Commission. Their joint statement admonished, "We cannot talk to the perpetrator of genocide before he has avowed his guilt."[22]

* * *

Attacks against TARC's Armenian members were discussed at the Commission's Istanbul meeting in September 2001. Genuinely concerned about the problems faced by TARC's Armenian members, Ilter Turkmen asked, "What can we do to help circumvent your difficulties?" TARC's Turkish members were wary of controversy and wanted to proceed slowly and cautiously. Sadi Erguvenc reflected, "We have been too ambitious. We cannot come up with concrete benefits in 48 hours." Ilter explained, "We look at this as a long process. It took the Greek-Turkish Forum several years to start developing policy recommendations."[23]

Turks believe that the genocide issue is an academic debate to be resolved by experts and historians. Some Turks called for opening of the Ottoman archives and establishment of a joint commission to conduct research. They proposed building a common monument to Armenians and Turks killed in Anatolia. Mehmet Ali Birand urged the Turkish government to "Openly announce that there was a civil war during which both parties had human losses, and that Turkey regrets what happened. Apologize if necessary. There is no need to fear apologies."[24] However, the Turkish establishment preferred to behave as if nothing happened, and insist there were no massacres of Armenians or that Armenians committed genocide against Turks. Turkish TARC members were also uncompromising. They resisted use of the term "genocide" in TARC documents. Even during informal off-the-record discussions, they would refer to the events as "mass killings" or the "mutual tragedy." To them using the word meant admitting the fact.

Both sides maintained a consistent position on the genocide issue. Reflecting the Turkish view, Ilter stated, "The Commission's task is not to come up with a historical judgment. As the dialogue proceeds, we hope to be able to overcome problems, but that does not mean that we will pass judgment on what happened 85 years ago."[25]

While the Armenians wanted TARC to address the genocide, they would not countenance discussion on the veracity of events. Van insisted, "This is not a 'historical commission' and there is no debate about the validity of the Armenian genocide."[26]

At the Istanbul meeting, Van explained that TARC's Armenian members had been accused of being manipulated to defer genocide recognition. He reaffirmed his hope that TARC would create a safe environment where Turks and Armenians could interact without fear of reprisal. Consistent with Track Two methodology, he hoped TARC could still serve as a context for developing new understanding and ideas, and that its insights could be transferred to decision makers and influence public opinion. Alex emphasized that TARC must be goal oriented. "We should come up with ideas and say things that governments cannot."[27]

The intense criticism had radicalized the Armenians. Speaking of his father from Mush and his mother from Kars, Andranik pointed out that "Just like millions of other Armenians, they became refugees and lost everything—the Motherland, relatives, friends, property." Andranik insisted that "Recognition of the genocide must have some material and territorial consequences. These include the building of memorials in major cities and where mass killings occurred, and symbolic territorial concessions such as the return of Armenians to Ararat and Ani."[28] To avoid further speculation, he insisted that TARC include language in its joint statement indicating that "[We] agree to discuss the Armenian genocide." The Turks flatly rejected his proposal.[29]

* * *

Though the Armenian Assembly of America (AAA) had succeeded in getting a textbook definition of genocide included in President George W. Bush's statement on April 24, 2001, the Dashnaks were livid that the actual word "genocide" was omitted. They charged that the Armenian Assembly had discouraged Congressman George Radanovich (R-CA) from reintroducing the genocide resolution. In a blatant effort to win supporters and increase financial contributions, the Armenian Revolutionary Federation

(ARF) accused TARC and the Armenian Assembly of being stooges of the U.S. government.

A nasty comic appeared in the ARF newspaper implying that the AAA was paid off by the State Department. It depicted an American official and an Armenian Assembly representative seated together at the "reconciliation table." A bag of money was being transferred under the table while the two toasted. The Dashnaks convinced some of their contacts on Capitol Hill to request that the Congressional Research Service (CRS) investigate TARC's financing. The CRS report concluded:

> The Department provided financial assistance to support the Commission's activities as it does other civil society initiatives or people-to-people contacts. The funds were in the form of a grant to American University (AU) for a conflict resolution program, which is supporting activities of the Commission. The State Department does not direct the American University's conflict resolution program. Although the State Department is committed to moving the reconciliation effort forward, it recognizes that minimal U.S. government involvement would probably be beneficial.[30]

In response to the report, Armenian National Committee of America chairman Ken Hachikian said, "Sadly this revelation only compounds [concerns about] the State Department's long-standing complicity in Turkey's denials of the Armenian genocide."[31] The ARF's Aghvan Vartanian claimed that "Putting international recognition of the Armenian genocide into oblivion is part of a common Turkish-American approach."[32]

TARC's critics also raised concern about my consulting arrangement with the State Department. Their press smeared me and questioned my impartiality.

Some of TARC's direct costs were indeed paid for out of the State Department grant to American University. At no time, however, were TARC members compensated. In fact, I am convinced that TARC's Armenian members were actually deprived of opportunity as a result of their participation. The State Department never interfered in my work as chairman of TARC. Once the grant was made, U.S. officials were interested in progress but took a completely hands-off approach.

Dashnaks may have had genuine policy concerns, but I believe they resented TARC because they were excluded from its activities. A few days after TARC was announced, the ARF Bureau objected to the participation of "unsanctioned individuals" and leveled harsh criticism against TARC's "self-appointed" members.[33] At a dinner in my honor hosted by John Ordway, America's ambassador to Armenia in June 2004, Vazgen Manukian of the National Democratic Union indicated that TARC would have been "more acceptable" to the Armenian public if it had a broader and more representative composition.[34]

Critics also raised questions about the credentials of Turkish TARC members, especially those seen as agents of Turkey's establishment. I selected TARC's Turkish members precisely because of who they were and what they represented. The involvement of establishment figures was necessary to break the taboo on Turkish-Armenian dialogue and fend off hard-liners. If TARC hoped to influence Turkish policy, it needed participants with access to the Turkish foreign ministry, the Turkish General Staff, and the National Security Council. I did not, however, include Turks like Omer Lutem and Mumtaz Soysal. For the same reason, I excluded Dashnaks. The participation of extremists would have obviated any chance for constructive dialogue. We neglected, however, to develop a strategy for neutralizing hard-line opponents. Briefing them regularly or including some as occasional observers might have clarified misunderstanding and mollified their criticism.

Critics found petty reasons to deprecate TARC. They complained about the unequal number of Turks and Armenians. TARC's name was the object of gratuitous scorn. Some asked why the Turks were mentioned first. They also objected to the term "commission," which implied something formal and official.

Van reiterated that TARC was not established to speak on behalf of all Armenians. "We certainly recognize the need to include others and intend to do so. We are open to including those who fit the commission's criteria. The process is explicitly intended to be flexible."[35] He continued, "As a working matter, the four of us match up with the six of them. As a matter of appearance, we understand that it is better if the sides are equal."[36] I worked with Van to develop the initial criteria for membership. The four Armenian TARC members were selected because of their significant international and national political experience, fluency in English, and willingness to work as part of a team. Van maintained that "We are not presently aware of anyone within the ARF/ANCA ranks who can meet the criteria for membership. We are open to discuss the matter, but their official reaction clearly confirms our judgment."[37]

TARC was also criticized as a secret process lacking transparency. The confidential nature of the process led to suspicions about what was happening. But until a decision was made to institutionalize the work by creating TARC, it was imperative to keep the initial meetings confidential. Though confidentiality gave rise to concerns about a conspiracy to sell out genocide recognition, it was necessary to achieve a critical mass before critics tried to kill the initiative. TARC would have been more favorably received had we maintained confidentiality a bit longer and tied the announcement to Ankara's decision to normalizing visa procedures for Armenian passport holders traveling to Turkey.

Many Armenians pledged support, but then backed off in the face of vocal opposition and intimidation. Vartan Oskanian was particularly disappointing. Instead of publicly endorsing the initiative, which Oskanian had committed to do, the Armenian government got nervous about being associated with TARC. Efforts to distance itself backfired by fueling even more intense criticism from political opponents.

On July 13, 2001, the Armenian foreign ministry spokeswoman said,

> First, I unequivocally state that the Ministry of Foreign Affairs of the Republic of Armenia has nothing to do with the establishment and activities of this 'Reconciliation Commission.' The Ministry of Foreign Affairs was only informed about this process, just like it gets informed about the activities of nearly all non-governmental organizations. As for the inclusion of Armenia's former Ambassador to Syria David Hovhanissian in the mentioned Commission, I'd remind you that in September 2000 he took up a lecturer's position at Yerevan State University.[38]

David Hovhanissian retorted, "Not only did the official leadership have no objections, it supported the idea. It was expected that the leadership would take up the mission of informing the society by explaining the meaning, aims, and content of the commission."[39] Andranik insisted that "The Armenian government was fully informed about TARC. Allegations that it had been created behind its back are simply not true." Van added, "There is no question that we were in constant contact with the government."[40] The Associated Press reported, "The reconciliation commission has no official status, but members said neither Turkey nor Armenia had objected to the meeting taking place."[41]

When blamed for handing over the conduct of Turkish-Armenian relations to TARC's Armenian members, the Armenian foreign ministry insisted that "This initiative could not replace direct state level contacts aimed at solving the conflict."[42] This was consistent with TARC's position all along. Van repeatedly stated, "TARC is not a substitute for government-to-government relations. We do not pretend in any way to do the work governments should do."[43]

Smelling blood, Dashnaks called for Oskanian's resignation on the grounds that he was aware of the initiative but did not inform Robert Kocharian. In response, the president's spokesman confirmed that "Kocharian knew about the Turkish-Armenian initiative and did not object to the commission's creation."[44]

Instead of being evaluated on its merits, TARC got caught up in a partisan political battle dating back to the presidency of Levon Ter-Petrossian. As a landlocked state, Armenia's economic progress and political stability have always depended on good neighborly relations. Ter-Petrossian came to power as a nationalist, but once in office he pursued a course of moderation. He broke ground by favoring normal relations with Turkey, but Ankara did not reciprocate. In response, the Armenian parliament insisted that Armenia's Declaration of Independence state, "The Republic of Armenia supports efforts to achieve international recognition of the Armenian genocide."

Following the uncovering of a coup attempt, Ter-Petrossian banned the ARF on December 28, 1994. ARF then intensified its worldwide campaign against Ter-Petrossian. When forces finally succeeded in forcing Ter-Petrossian to resign in 1998, Kocharian, the hard-line former prime minister of the "Republic of Nagorno-Karabakh," became president of Armenia. In return for their political support, Kocharian lifted the banning of ARF. Though the government of Armenia has never made any claim on Turkey's territory, Dashnaks have territorial ambitions and refuse to recognize the territorial integrity of Turkey. They believe that Armenia should fight for its historic rights, including claims on territory in eastern Turkey.

TARC's opponents were particularly riled by the inclusion of Alex. To Dashnaks, Alex was a living embodiment of Ter-Petrossian's failed efforts at accommodation. Alex resigned as foreign minister when Ter-Petrossian stepped down, leaving office with a reputation for integrity, loyalty, and commitment to democracy. Though some media outlets raised concerns about Alex's participation, Sargis Matcharian wrote, "Let us resort to wisdom and the benefit of silence, let us restrain our tongues and our pens, let us stop the noise, gossips and squabbling and let the knowledgeable members of the Reconciliation Commission, who are as patriotic and committed as we are, do their noble work."[45] Later Alex was mugged in Yerevan and beaten to a pulp.

When TARC was announced, the *Washington Times* commended "the governments of Armenia and Turkey [for showing] courage in tacitly endorsing the reconciliation commission. The political cost of holding such a commission could be high, given the hostility the people of both countries feel towards each other."[46] But Kocharian was hedging his bets. He maintained, "If Turkey continues denying the past, our reconciliation will remain hostage to distrust."[47] Oskanian was also planning contingencies. "If the process breaks down, we could use that to show the United States and other countries that Turkey is unable to address problems through such dialogues and that international recognition is the only way out."[48]

TARC's Armenian members issued a statement on August 1, 2001. "The announcement of a private Turkish-Armenian Reconciliation Commission has already opened new possibilities for Armenians and Turks. From around the world, most Armenians have offered support, both publicly and privately. They share with us the belief that if Armenians and Turks can talk directly and in a structured fashion addressing the numerous issues that divide us, some progress may follow." Van maintained that "Armenian-Americans get what TARC is all about."[49] At Van's request I met with Hrair Hovnanian and Robert Kaloosdian, leaders of the AAA. Hovnanian was in a big hurry to see results. I explained that we were working on Ankara to lift restrictions for Armenian passport holders to enter Turkey and reestablishing high-level diplomatic contacts. Hovnanian and Kaloosdian pushed for dates and deliverables. I pushed back. Neither Track Two nor official diplomacy works that way.

Claiming it was losing members and contributions, the AAA issued a statement on December 1, 2001, distancing itself from TARC. "The AAA is no longer involved with TARC. Should individuals affiliated with the Assembly choose to participate in the re-activated TARC, they will be doing so in their private capacity and not as a representative of the Assembly."[50] Despite the AAA's nervousness over its association with TARC, it turned out that it actually gained members and contributions during this period. The Assembly only lost support when it prematurely withdrew its support from TARC.

Soon thereafter, Van stepped down as AAA chairman to work more intensively on TARC. Recognizing that the embargo is impoverishing Armenia and driving its youth into the Diaspora, he and the other TARC members persisted in their dialogue with Turks. On April 24, 2003, their vision and valor were acknowledged by George W. Bush, who said, "Transcending this venomous pattern requires painful introspection about the past and wise determination to forge a new future based on truth and reconciliation." He saluted "wise and bold friends from Armenia and Turkey who are coming together in a spirit of reconciliation to consider these events."[51]

Notes

1. *Armenian Radio Hour of New Jersey,* October 17, 2001.
2. Ibid.
3. *Turkish Daily News,* July 12, 2001.
4. Sargis Matcharian, "Let Us Just Once Really Pay Homage to Our Martyrs," *Kach Nazar Magazine,* August 1, 2001.
5. *The Gazette,* April 23, 2002.
6. *Armenian Radio Hour of New Jersey,* October 17, 2001.
7. *Radio Free Europe,* June 13, 2002.
8. Primate, Diocesan Council, August 24, 2001.
9. *Azat Artsakh,* July 24, 2001.
10. Statement by the Armenian Assembly of America, July 10, 2001.
11. *The Armenian Weekly,* February/March, 2002.
12. *Armenian Radio Hour of New Jersey,* October 17, 2001.

13. *Radio Free Europe,* December 12, 2001.
14. FAAE press release, December 18, 2001.
15. George Aghjayan, "A Reconciliation Based on Denial," *Armenian Weekly,* July 21–27, 2001.
16. *California Courier,* November 1, 2001.
17. *Armenian Weekly,* May 11–17, 2002.
18. Conference of the Assembly of Turkish American Associations, November 2, 2001.
19. Meeting notes, September 24, 2003.
20. *Mirror Spectator,* October 17, 2001.
21. Meeting notes, September 24, 2001.
22. Congressional Research Service, October 2, 2001.
23. Meeting notes, September 24, 2001.
24. Mehmet Ali Birand, *Posta,* April 27, 2001.
25. Kemal Ilter, "A Historic Step for Both Turks and Armenians," *Turkish Daily News,* July 12, 2001.
26. *Armenian Radio Hour of New Jersey,* October 17, 2001.
27. Meeting notes, September 24, 2001.
28. Meeting notes, September 21, 2001.
29. Meeting notes, September 24, 2001.
30. Congressional Research Service, October 2, 2001.
31. Radio Free Europe, October 16, 2001.
32. *Asbarez On-line,* April 23, 2002.
33. ARF Statement, July 13, 2001.
34. *Asbarez On-line,* April 23, 2002.
35. *Focus,* August 8, 2001.
36. *Armenian Radio Hour of New Jersey,* October 16, 2001.
37. *Probe,* August 8, 2001.
38. Statement by Dziunik Aghajanian, Armenian Ministry of Foreign Affairs, July 13, 2001.
39. Armenian News Network, April 16, 2002.
40. *Armenpress,* February 6, 2002.
41. "Turkish and Armenian Figures Establish Reconciliation Commission," Associated Press, July 11, 2001.
42. Statement by Dziunik Aghajanian, Armenian Ministry of Foreign Affairs, July 13, 2001.
43. *The Armenian Weekly,* February/March, 2002.
44. Radio Free Europe, July 14, 2001.
45. Sargis Matcharian, "Let Us Just Once Really Pay Homage to Our Martyrs," *Kach Nazar Magazine,* August 1, 2001.
46. "Turkish Armenian Reconciliation," *The Washington Times,* July 17, 2001.
47. *Arminfo,* May 2, 2002.
48. *Armenia Report,* July 24, 2001.
49. *Mirror Spectator,* October 17, 2001.
50. AAA Statement, December 1, 2001.
51. The White House, April 24, 2003.

Ilter Turkmen, Turkey's former foreign minister and a TARC member. (AP/World Wide Photos)

Van Z. Krikorian, a founding TARC member. (AP/Wide World Photos)

TARC's founding members. (AP/Wide World Photos)

7

LET A HUNDRED FLOWERS BLOOM

TARC broke the ice and helped catalyze a wide array of civil society Track Two activities. It was also a lightning rod for criticism, thereby enabling other civil society initiatives to proceed "under the radar." Though people-to-people contacts cannot solve core political problems, they can help prepare the ground for negotiations. When a critical mass of the polity demands change, public pressure can force politicians to alter their approach. The impact of civil society is especially significant in democracies where officials are responsive to public opinion and ultimately accountable to the electorate.

American University's (AU) *Track Two Program on Turkey and the Caucasus* started as a modest endeavor. The State Department's Bureau of Educational and Cultural Affairs (ECA) transferred small sums to the American embassy in Vienna, which in turn would make grants to the Diplomatic Academy. Funds were used to pay the travel and in-country costs of the first Vienna meetings.

Helena Finn returned to Washington, D.C., and was serving as the Acting Assistant Secretary of State for Educational and Cultural Affairs. When collaboration with the Turkish History Foundation became unworkable, Helena played an important role securing Sabanci University as a project partner. Helena's interest in Turkey never waned despite her new global responsibilities. Instead of approaching the process piecemeal, Helena wanted to know what would be required to conduct a comprehensive Track Two program involving Turks and Armenians.

As part of its official development assistance, the U.S. Congress authorizes funds annually to consolidate democratic development of the Newly Independent States (NIS). Under the chairmanship of Van Krikorian, the Armenian Assembly of America made sure that Armenia benefited handsomely from resources made available to NIS countries through the Freedom Support Act (FSA). As a result of its efforts, Armenia became the third largest per capita recipient of U.S. foreign assistance behind Israel and Egypt.

Before moving to Afghanistan to oversee reconstruction assistance after the Taliban was overthrown, Ambassador William Taylor administered FSA funds as well as the congressional allocation for Securing Eastern European Democracies (SEED). Ambassador Taylor was enthusiastic about Track Two and complimentary of our progress catalyzing a dialogue between Turks and Armenians. Turkey fell between the cracks of geographically defined grant assistance programs administered by the U.S. Agency for International Development (USAID). It was not a recipient of assistance via FSA or SEED. Taylor asked if we could widen the scope of our program to include Azerbaijan. Including Azerbaijan would solve a bureaucratic problem and enable grant funds to be drawn from the FSA account.

I was wary of including Azerbaijan. In 1995, I traveled to the Caucasus on behalf of the International Peace Research Institute, Oslo. My assignment was to organize an initiative on regional economic cooperation involving representatives from Turkey, Armenia, Azerbaijan, and Georgia. It looked like arrangements were in order, until the Azeri delegation pulled out at the last minute. PRIO frantically tried to notify participants before they traveled to Norway, but some were already en route and arrived to attend a meeting that never took place.

Taylor persuaded me to visit Azerbaijan and explore Track Two project opportunities. I reached out to Leila Alieva, an old friend from Moscow State University with whom I had collaborated in the past. Leila is a brilliant Azeri analyst who has experience with Armenians. She warned me that Azeri civil society had little interest in engaging their Armenian counterparts. To talk about normalization meant accepting the status quo. As long as Azeri territory was occupied in Nagorno-Karabakh, Track Two would be extremely difficult.

In 1998, the Organization for Security and Cooperation in Europe (OSCE) had reinvigorated its efforts to secure a final peace agreement for the conflict. The OSCE Minsk Group, which includes Russia, France, and the United States, took the lead in negotiations. Leila was hopeful that America's more active role would be the key to progress. Though discouraged by their government, some Azeris were prepared to engage in Track Two. They were more ready upon learning that funds were available.

The State Department briefed me on the Minsk Group negotiations. The Caucasus coordinator was upbeat about prospects for a settlement in early 2001. Secretary of State Colin Powell was planning to invite Robert Kocharian and Azerbaijan's president Haider Aliev for talks at Key

West, Florida. Despite the rosy prognosis, I was cautious. So were Taylor and other old hands at the State Department. If a deal was negotiated ending the Nagorno-Karabakh conflict, Track Two activities between Azeris and Armenians could help consolidate the agreement. If the negotiations stalled, Track Two would be a safety net cushioning negative implications.

I approached Professor Abdul Aziz Said at American University with a unique offer. The State Department would make $3 million available. A flexible institution was needed to manage subcontracts with dozens of project partners in Turkey, Armenia, and Azerbaijan. Was Aziz's Center for Global Peace at American University able to manage the task?

An American of Syrian descent, Said is a well-respected and accomplished academician with decades of Track Two experience. An imposing figure with flowing white hair and sharp aquiline features, Said appreciated the significance of the State Department's offer. He agreed that the Center for Global Peace would administer the grant. The grant agreement was finalized just hours before TARC's announcement in Geneva on July 9, 2001.

American University's Track Two program focused on contact and cooperation between Turkish and Armenian and between Azeri and Armenian civil society representatives. The portfolio was guided by three rules. First, every project must be jointly administered by non-governmental organizations (NGOs) in the target countries. Second, project partners had to be transparent in their use of funds. Third, AU staff or international specialists would be assigned to assist project management and provide technical advice. Most project partners never sought information on AU's funding, nor were they aware of a link between their activities and TARC.

TARC's announcement shattered the taboo surrounding Turkish-Armenian dialogue. Suddenly it seemed that every Turkish and Armenian NGO was clamoring for contact. AU was perfectly positioned to assist key NGOs. It emphasized collaborative ventures between groups with the ability to influence public opinion. Activities focused on culture, media, economy, education, gender issues and leadership development. AU placed a premium on influencing policy by involving parliamentarians, mayors, and local officials from bordering provinces in Turkey and Armenia.

* * *

Initial activities focused on culture. The goal was to emphasize the human dimension and, as a result, to personalize Turkish-Armenian relations. I also anticipated that cultural events would generate positive media coverage in both countries, which was indeed the case.

The Ankara String Quartet, an official ensemble of the Turkish government, had performed all over the world but never in Armenia. OCTA

Records invited them to Yerevan and the Ankara String Quartet was
included in the Christian Armenia 1700 classical music festival. The musicians requested scores of Armenian music, which they practiced and
performed in Yerevan's historic concert hall. As official guests of Armenia, they were also hosted by the Catholicos of the Armenian Apostolic
Church at its headquarters in Echmiadzin. Given security concerns, AU
hired bodyguards for the Turkish musicians.

The following spring, Armenia's Komitas Quartet performed in Istanbul and Antalya returning the visit of the Ankara String Quartet to Yerevan. After the performance, Komitas was surprised that no flowers were
given to the performers. Giving floral bouquets after a musical performance is a tradition in Armenia. However, this is not the case in Turkey
particularly if the performers are men. Though the Turkish hosts wanted
to honor the Armenian tradition, they thought that presenting flowers
might be misunderstood by the Turkish audience. To satisfy the protocol
requirements of both sides, the Turkish hosts deftly came up with a solution. They arranged for twenty-five children to come on stage and present bouquets to the Armenian performers. The performance culminated in
a soulful cello duet of cellists from Komitas and the Ankara String Quartet.

In addition to classical music concerts, Lalezar, the Turkish folk music
group, was sponsored to perform in Istanbul and Yerevan with Richard
Hagopian, an Armenian-American who is famous for his performance of
traditional Armenian music. Dashnaks tried to disrupt the concert with
loud protests and placards. A stink bomb was thrown into the concert
hall. Despite the disruption, the audience insisted that the performance
take place. Many Armenians expressed embarrassment and remorse for
the incident in interviews outside the concert hall after the performance.
When Richard Hagopian joined Lalezar for performances in Turkey, Hagopian addressed the audience and local media in fluent in Turkish. Using
his language skills and warm personality to endear the Turkish audience,
Hagopian exemplified the skills of a true cultural ambassador.

Richard Hagopian invited Turkish musicians to join his ensemble to
perform as part of the Boston World Music series, and at the Smithsonian
Institute's Sackler Museum. The concerts profiled the work of Udi Hrant,
the famous Turkish-Armenian musician from Istanbul who specialized
in a traditional instrument called the "oud." After the Yerevan incident,
I was concerned that Dashnaks in the Diaspora would organize protests
outside the Smithsonian. Fortunately, the concerts went off without a
glitch. Turkish-Americans and Armenian-Americans held hands and
swayed to the music during the encore.

The concerts and other cultural events were widely reported in both
Turkish and Armenian mainstream media. In addition, documentaries

about the string quartets and the folk music concerts were produced by Tigran Xmalian, director of the Yerevan Film Studio. The film will be distributed to Turkish, Armenian, and U.S. television stations. Cultural events had the desired effect by generating positive media coverage and helping to reduce negative stereotypes.

Other cultural activities included restoration of Akhtamar Church. Built on an island in the middle of Lake Van, Akhtamar is one of the most holy ancient Armenian monasteries. An international group of restoration and architectural experts from the Land and Culture Organization traveled to Istanbul and Van in eastern Turkey to assess prospects for restoring and reconsecrating the Akhtamar Church. Follow-up meetings with Turkish, Armenian, and international restoration experts were held in New York. After two years of delicate negotiations, representatives from both the Turkish and Armenian Ministries of Culture agreed to meet in an "unofficial" capacity. The Istanbul meeting was organized by the Historic Heritage Protection Foundation. The group also traveled to Akhtamar with Turkish, Armenian, and Diaspora experts to assess restoration requirements for the church's stonework and celebrated frescos. Turkish and Turkish-Armenian students were involved. Their initiative was called "Restoring Our Souls Through Restoration of a Church."

Media activities started with a splash. I arranged for Mehmet Ali Birand, CNN Turk's ace anchorman, to visit Yerevan and interview President Robert Kocharian. During the historic interview, Kocharian vowed that the Republic of Armenia would not make territorial claims or seek financial reparations. Over the next several years, CNN Turk broadcast news on Turkish-Armenian relations and Mehmet Ali Birand hosted several interviews and talk shows on the subject.

Journalists with an interest in Turkish-Armenian relations were invited to participate in a journalist exchange program. Leading Turkish journalists wrote about their trip to Armenia and Nagorno-Karabakh. Coverage included news items as well as human interest stories. Armenian journalists from the Yerevan Press Club visited Istanbul and several Turkish papers reprinted editorials written by Armenian columnists.

Another exchange program targeted young up-and-coming Turkish and Armenian journalists. Turks met government officials, visited cultural sites, and held discussions with newspaper, television, and radio staff in Armenia. During the Armenians' reciprocal trip, there was a political crisis and Prime Minister Bulent Ecevit resigned. Being in Turkey at the time provided an exciting opportunity to interview Turkish political analysts, academics, parliamentarians, and business leaders. The journalists also participated in a workshop on conflict resolution media techniques organized by Common Ground Productions.

A new women's magazine was launched. Supervised by Sule Kilicar-slan, who would come to play a key role expanding air travel between Turkey and Armenia, and an editorial board of Turkish and Armenian women, the glossy was published in Armenian, Turkish, and English. The magazine highlighted successful women as role models. Other topics included health, culture, cuisine, and fashion. Fifteen thousand copies were sold or distributed in Turkey, Armenia, France, Germany, and the United States. An online electronic version was also posted on the Web.

To foster cooperation between Turkish and Armenian women's groups, a delegation of Turkish women traveled to Yerevan to celebrate International Women's Day on March 8, 2002. Hranus Hratyan of the Armenian Women's Group organized meetings with women parliamentarians, business leaders, and academics, as well as a panel discussion at Yerevan State University. Tensions arose at a press briefing when the Armenian women raised the subject of the Armenian genocide. During a reciprocal trip to Istanbul, the Marmara Foundation disconnected the public address system when Hranus was giving a speech about the genocide. Despite this unfortunate event, the women's groups continued their collaboration. Their next meeting proceeded without incident thanks to AU's Rachel Pentlarge, who helped mediate differences. A series of meetings between women parliamentarians also ensued.

The Turkish-Armenian Business Development Council (TABDC) was a solid partner on several ventures. Ahmet Ertegun, the respected founder and chairman of Atlantic Records, agreed to serve as honorary chair of the advisory board. Its Istanbul representative, Noyan Soyak, proved particularly adept at project management. His brother, Kaan, was energetic in pursuing both business and cultural activities promoting Turkish-Armenian rapprochement.

The Virtual Agricultural Wholesale Market (VAWM) was established by TABDC and the International Center for Human Development (ICHD) in Armenia. Serving as an information clearinghouse, its database helps farmers in northwestern Armenia and eastern Turkey access information on harvest forecasts, market surveys, seed, fertilizer and pesticide, and agricultural machinery. The Web site evolved into the Marketing Network of the Caucasus (MANEC), a virtual forum promoting sales for a range of goods. Trade delegations were exchanged and plans made for a regional trade fair and a regional chamber of commerce.

Academic activities were organized by the Turkish Economic and Social Studies Foundation (TESEV) and the Armenian Sociological Association (ASA). To assess mutual perceptions of Turks by Armenians and of Armenians by Turks, the organizations developed a joint methodology, undertook fieldwork in both countries, and presented findings at an international seminar. Ruben Safrastyan, a professor at Yerevan State University and director of the Turkish Studies Department at Armenia's National Academy of Sciences Institute of Oriental Studies, initiated academic contacts with counterparts at Bilkent University and Sabanci University.

In addition to NGO constituencies, Track Two targeted policy-makers. A Turkish-Armenian parliamentary exchange was launched at the Annual Forum of Parliamentarians for Global Action (PGA) in Sweden. Participants focused on economic issues, including energy and transport. They explored Silk Road reconstruction, regional infrastructure, energy pipelines, and opportunities for Armenia to export electricity to Turkey. The parliamentary group endorsed normal travel and trade between the two countries. The initiative set the stage for official efforts to establish a Turkish-Armenian Parliamentary Commission.

Mayors, chambers of commerce, and civic leaders from bordering Turkish and Armenian provinces participated in capacity-building workshops for local government officials. The (Turkish) Center for the Research of Societal Problems (TOSAM) and Armenia's ICHD developed a joint curriculum in mediation, cross-cultural communication, and collaborative problem solving. More than five hundred local leaders in Armenia and Turkey participated in the training. Armenians and Turks also met to compare lessons learned and establish an advocacy group on opening the border.

Though Diaspora leaders active in the Armenian Assembly of America and the Association of Turkish American Associations (ATAA) also explored joint activities, it proved much more difficult to foster collaboration between the Diaspora communities. Diaspora members are typically more hard-line. Having reaped the benefits from peace and prosperity, they have the luxury to assert uncompromising positions.

Track Two activities were formally welcomed by the Armenian government. On the occasion of my visit to Yerevan, the foreign ministry spokeswoman announced, "The Armenian authorities encourage contacts between various organizations and their Turkish colleagues."[1] Contact and cooperation were favorably viewed on both sides. The *Turkish Daily News* reported that "People to people contacts are paving the way for second steps between Ankara and Yerevan."[2]

Exchanges were not always easy. There were times when, without warning, Armenian hosts insisted that Turkish delegations visit the Armenian Genocide Memorial in Yerevan where they were photographed and asked to write their thoughts in a memorial book maintained by the museum. Turks faced a conundrum. Some did not want a visit to the memorial to imply recognition of the genocide. On the other hand, they did not want to refuse lest it be construed as disrespect by their hosts. Such instances were rare and, for the most part, exchange programs went off without a hitch.

* * *

Track Two between Armenians and Azeris was even more difficult than between Armenians and Turks. President Haider Aliev actively discouraged Track Two activities and the Azerbaijan parliament passed legislation forbidding it. Despite these constraints, some Armenian-Azeri activities were successfully undertaken.

TOSAM and ICHD applied their curriculum in collaborative problem solving in workshops for Azeris and Karabakh Armenians. After a series of training programs, participants met to evaluate the project and propose several joint task forces, including a women's group. Other joint projects are being explored, such as land mine awareness and youth education in conflict areas. A media group was also established to monitor reporting and organize joint documentaries. Parallel activities were merged whenever possible.

Armenian and Azeri sociologists worked together to research mutual perceptions. One thousand persons from each country were surveyed. The findings, including an assessment of prospects and obstacles to improved relations, were disseminated in academic circles and via Azeri and Armenian media. Displaced persons from Nagorno-Karabakh were also involved.

The International Rescue Committee (IRC) conducted a peace education program for youth in displacement camps. After "training trainers," 120 Azeris participated in a workshop with peace educators. An Azeri university student joined the training team in order to develop a local capability for transferring training techniques to other regions in Azerbaijan. To evaluate the project, Pentlarge visited a camp in Latchin. The meeting occurred at a run-down old schoolhouse with concrete floors, dilapidated desks, and an ancient chalkboard. When the students entered, they were all scrubbed and wearing their best clothes with shoes polished and hair neatly combed. In a poignant testimony to the IRC's good work, they expressed gratitude for the project and explained how the training helped make them more responsible members of their family and community and future leaders of their country.

Azeri and Armenian members of parliament met in Sweden under the auspices of PGA. The seminar was facilitated by Senator Longin Pastusiak, president of the Polish Senate, and Senator John Connor of Ireland. A Swedish expert on water and natural resource management worked with Azeri and Armenian partners to assess conditions and then escorted a joint delegation to Johannesburg where they attended the UN Summit on Sustainable Development. A follow-up seminar on collaborative water resource management was hosted at the Diplomatic Academy of Vienna. Armenian and Azeri parliamentarians were eventually integrated into the overall activities of PGA.

Armenians and Azeris found that they had much in common. Both speak Russian and share a common history of struggle against communism. However, the presidents of Armenia and Azerbaijan were both impediments to their country's democratic development. Many Armenians and Azeris were not able or willing to defy their authorities and participate in Armenian-Azeri Track Two activities. In these instances, parallel activities were pursued or a multilateral approach was used. Though meetings with Armenians, Azeris, Georgians, and Turks presented additional logistical challenges, the multilateral framework enabled contact to occur that led to more enduring cooperation.

A group of universities in the region—Baku State University and Khazar University in Azerbaijan, Tbilisi State University and the Tbilisi Institute of Asia and Africa in Georgia, and Yerevan State University and Yerevan State Linguistic University in Armenia—established the Caucasus International Consortium for Academic Cooperation (CICAC). Sabanci University and Middle East Technical University in Turkey also participated in the development of CICAC, as well as academic exchanges and collaborative research. Common courses on "The Culture of the Caucasus" and "The Caucasus in Global Perspective" were developed.

The Task Force on Regional Economic Integration included economists, business leaders and local government. It studied opportunities for regional economic integration focusing on infrastructure, transport, banking, taxes, and customs. In addition to a Web site providing information to traders and investors, the task force also developed plans for a South Caucasus Economic Union.

A working group of mayors from bordering provinces in Azerbaijan, Armenia, Georgia, and Turkey developed a regional development strategy. Training in local government administration was provided to participants came from Kars, Erzurum, Igdir, and Artvin (Turkey); Shirak, Lori, and Tavush (Armenia); Ghazak, Aghstafa, and Gyanja (Azerbaijan); Samkheti and Javakheti (Georgia). The Centre for Non-Traditional Conflict Resolution Methods took a leading role coordinating activities and encouraging local officials to work together.

All of AU's partners working on regional integration and economic development were brought together to make plans for a regional chamber of commerce. Appreciating the finite nature of AU's involvement, the Track Two program emphasized capacity building for local partners. To this end, AU worked with selected organizations to help them become self-sustaining and develop plans for future support from concerned governments, as well as private funders such as the Eurasia Foundation.

Track Two activities were well served by specialists who brought skill, patience, and perseverance to each endeavor. For example, Calvin Sims, an international correspondent for the *New York Times*, coordinated media exchanges. He and Shelley Hack, who set up the independent media in postwar Bosnia and Herzegovina, advised production of the women's magazine. George Terzis of the European Centre for Common Ground (ECCG) conducted conflict resolution media training. PGA's Shazia Rafi and Eva Dunn supported interparliamentary activities. Ed Blakely, dean of the Milano School of Management at the New School University, provided training to local government officials. Professor Mieke Meurs from American University's Department of Economics advised on regional economic integration.

Over a three-year period, professional staff at American University's Center for Global Peace worked exhaustively on day-to-day management. Great credit is due Betty Sitka and Rachel Pentlarge, who managed overall activities including project finance and administration. Every activity required significant guidance and care. Even seemingly simple tasks were fraught with unexpected difficulties that required troubleshooting. The AU staff was called upon to make judgment calls, and apply conflict resolution expertise for every project. Their skill, hard work, and dedication were indispensable to the program.

I provided Marc Grossman with an activities report on the Track Two Program on Turkey and the Caucasus. He responded, "I asked you to start a dialogue and you catalyzed a social movement."

Notes

1. Armenia News Network, April 18, 2002.
2. *Turkish Daily News,* April 24, 2002.

8

TERROR STRIKES

To the extent that Turkish-Armenian reconciliation was a goal of U.S. foreign policy, its importance diminished drastically after September 11, 2001. The fight against terrorism would redefine U.S.-Turkish relations and influence Turkey's relations in the Caucasus and Central Asia. September 11 had a profound impact on TARC's reconciliation efforts.

The Bush administration made clear that it would use all necessary and appropriate means to retaliate against terror groups, as well as regimes that harbor them. Despite its military might, the U.S. cannot fight terrorism alone. It relies on allies and strategic coalitions. Deputy Defense Secretary Paul Wolfowitz said, "To win the war against terrorism, we have to reach out to the hundreds of millions of moderate and tolerant people in the Muslim world. Turkey is crucial to bridging the dangerous gap between the West and the Muslim world." Wolfowitz went on to characterize Turkey as a "truly indispensable nation" whose "partnership with the United States has become even more important in the wake of the crisis that has gripped the world since September 11."[1]

When George W. Bush told countries "either you're with us or against us," Turkey, Armenia, and Azerbaijan all aligned themselves with the United States. Turkey sent troops to fight al Qaeda and the Taliban and ultimately assumed command of the International Security Assistance Force for Afghanistan. Robert Kocharian committed to confront "the evil of terrorism with determination and resolve." He also offered use of Armenia's airspace for coalition aircraft based at Incirlik Air Force Base in Turkey.[2] Azerbaijan also sent messages of support and facilitated the transport of supplies. In exchange for its participation, Baku petitioned the U.S. to lift Section 907 of the Freedom Support Act.

Though Azerbaijan was the clear loser in its war with ethnic Armenians, the U.S. Congress adopted Section 907 of the Freedom Support Act in 1992, which placed restrictions on assistance to Azerbaijan until it ceases "all blockades and other offensive uses of force against Armenia and Nagorno-Karabakh." Van Krikorian saw Section 907 as one of his greatest legislative accomplishments. After September 11, others disagreed. Zbigniew Brezinski, Brent Scowcoft, and Anthony Lake—three former national security advisors—wrote the Senate leadership urging the repeal of this "archaic sanction against Azerbaijan."[3] Businesses and oil companies also urged repeal, as did leading Jewish organizations. Senator Sam Brownback (R-KS), who led the fight for repeal, ultimately attained congressional authority for a presidential national security waiver. The authorizing legislation also affirmed Armenia's importance in the fight against terrorism and granted an additional $4.6 million in military assistance to Armenia.

In addition, Baku wanted America's help restoring its control over Nagorno-Karabakh. In August 2001, Colin Powell invited Kocharian and Haider Aliev to Key West for peace talks. It appeared they were close to a deal; Armenia would annex Nagorno-Karabakh plus the land mass that separated Nagorno-Karabakh from Armenia prior to the war. Armenia also would provide Azerbaijan with a corridor to Nakichevan through the Meghri region. The so-called Meghri swap would directly connect Azerbaijan and Nakichevan. All Azeris displaced by the conflict would have the right of return to nonannexed territories, and significant foreign aid would be provided to Azerbaijan paying for the reintegration or resettlement of Azeri refugees. Additional funds were also pledged to help sweeten the deal for Azerbaijan. Both presidents, however, were met by a firestorm of controversy when they went home. Neither had sufficiently prepared their polity for painful concessions.

Ankara still adhered to Turgut Ozal's commitment to Azerbaijan linking normalization of Turkey's relations with Armenia to the return of "occupied territories." During his official visit to Washington in January 2002, Prime Minister Bulent Ecevit reiterated that the normalization of Turkish-Armenian relations depended on a settlement of the Nagorno-Karabakh conflict. "If the occupation of Azerbaijani territory is ended, then we will be very glad to establish diplomatic relations with Armenia."[4]

About a million ethnic Azeris reside in Turkey. Using fraternal ties between Turks and Azeris and Azerbaijan's energy wealth to leverage Ankara's support for Azerbaijan, Aliev succeeded in convincing Ankara to blockade Armenia. By diminishing Armenia's economic capacity and undermining its self-reliance, Aliev hoped to force Armenia to negotiate from a weaker position and hence compel concessions. According to Vartan Oskanian, "Turkey closed down its borders with Armenia ten years ago under pressure from Azerbaijan. But what was expected did not materi-

alize. The main problem in the relationship between Turkey and Armenia is the pressure that Azerbaijan exerts on Turkey over the Karabakh
conflict."[5] He also stated, "Bilateral relations should not be taken hostage
by Azerbaijani-Armenian disputes and Turkey should not link the formation of ties with us to Azerbaijani issues."[6]

* * *

TARC's next meeting occurred during the volatile period after September 11. Schedules from Kennedy Airport were drastically curtailed and
virtually every seat on the flight was empty. Images of jetliners crashing
into the twin towers were still fresh in everyone's mind. Travelers were
also deterred by warnings of attacks against U.S. interests in Turkey. The
American embassy and consulates were on high alert. The Istanbul Hil-
ton had only ten other guests. The concierge, reception clerks, and shoe-
shine boy silently manned their posts.

The Turks came to the table bolstered by the knowledge that Turkey's indispensable role in the fight against terrorism gave them the upper hand.
September 11 forced TARC to recalibrate its approach. Andranik noted,
"Now no one will raise the genocide in Congress. Turkey has once again become a key country for implementation of America's strategic interests in
the Near East."[7] Ilter Turkmen expressed heartfelt regrets for America's tragedy. Gunduz Aktan was less considerate. "Now you know how we feel," referring to Turkey's decade-long struggle with the Kurdistan Worker's Party.

Getting down to business, TARC's Turkish members insisted that reconciliation be preceded by progress on core issues. They maintained that
the Armenian Diaspora was the most significant stumbling block. Discussions between Turks and Armenians would always revert to matters
concerning the genocide. Oskanian affirmed, "Troubled memories, a tortured past, recriminations, unsettled accounts and the enduring wounds
of victimization plague the national consciousness of [our] peoples."
They are like "old ghosts rattling in [the] closet."[8]

Other ghosts include the memory of slain Turkish diplomats. During
TARC's visit to Istanbul in September 2001, ASALA's crimes came up over
lunch at an elegant boathouse on the Bosphorus. Andranik Migranian
justified the assassinations, maintaining that ASALA's tactics were necessary to focus international attention on genocide recognition. Emin Mahir
Balcioglu tensed at Andranik's side. As a young boy, Emin Mahir returned
from school one day to discover that his father, Turkey's ambassador in
Madrid, had been murdered by ASALA. Overcoming the anger of his
loss, Emin Mahir would later join TARC and become active in cultural cooperation as a vehicle for reconciliation. Van Krikorian reflected, "It was
significant that we met people affected by Armenian terrorism in Turkey
and yet they harbored no ill will."[9]

TARC never tried to negotiate whether the genocide did or did not occur, nor did it undertake an unofficial dialogue exploring a settlement of the Karabakh dispute. Instead it focused on practical forms of cooperation. When H.R. 596 was introduced in 2000, Ankara protested by imposing visa restrictions on Armenians traveling to Turkey. Visas could not be secured at the point of entry; they could only be issued by Turkish embassies or consulates. The absence of diplomatic facilities in Armenia posed a problem. It also complicated arrangements for Armenian guest workers in Turkey. As many as 40,000 Armenians work in Turkey and send money home to their families.

TARC called on Ankara to lift its restrictions and normalize the visa regime. On January 10, 2002, Turkey finally implemented new procedures enabling Armenians to get a visa at any border point rather than being required to obtain one before arrival. With the restrictions removed, Armenians from Armenia no longer have to fly to Moscow, Tbilisi, or another city with a Turkish consulate to obtain a visa. Now they can get one at the Istanbul airport for $15 that allows them to stay for up to three months. The new procedure had a significant impact on 40,000 Armenians who make their living in Turkey; Ankara described the amended procedure as a "goodwill gesture."

Ustun Erguder maintained that "Abolition of visa restrictions was the first fruit of TARC's efforts. My colleagues who are former ambassadors were very influential in getting this done."[10] Gunduz's efforts to persuade the national security establishment were praiseworthy. Marc Grossman also helped by raising the matter in numerous discussions with Turkish counterparts.

* * *

As a first step toward opening the border, TARC endorsed resuming railroad services between Kars and Gyumri, which were suspended in 1993. Though the two cities are only 90 km apart, the border is sealed and heavily militarized. Officially, there is no trade between Turkey and Armenia, but goods circulate between the two countries via Georgia. Union of Manufacturers and Businessmen in Armenia estimates the value of illegal trade at $100 million each year.

The U.S. Trade and Development Agency conducted a technical study in 1999–2000 on the "Trans-Caucasus Rail Project," which evaluated the physical condition of both the northern and southern trans-Caucasus routes emanating from Kars. The study found that the rail link was considerably degraded due to neglect, the blockade, and the earthquake. In addition, 22 km of track near Imlishi in Nagorno-Karabakh had been torn up. The study also recommended 13 km of new track near Gyumri. In addition to reelectrification, it proposed installing a line switch for the grade transition between Turkey and Armenia. Ballast, ties, and rail would also be needed. So would at least two new bridges.

The U.S. Agency for International Development offered to pay for upgrading the system in Armenia. The European Bank for Reconstruction and Development offered financing for rail line renovation via the Transport Corridor Europe–Caucasus–Asia program. The EU also offered to assist. Later, U.S. officials emphasized the need for rail transport to deliver materials to troops in Afghanistan, but Ankara still refused to open the Kars-Gyumri gate.

Severing direct trade ties with Armenia had a big impact on economic conditions in eastern Anatolia. Mehmet Yilmaz, president of the Kars chamber of commerce, indicated, "We want to open the border. It will mean jobs for everyone. Armenians will visit Kars to buy foodstuffs and textiles. Turkish products such as butter, jam and olive oil are being sent to Georgia and Iran and then resold in Armenia. Both sides are eager to resume direct trade."[11] After his visit to Kars, Ustun observed, "the city is dying."[12]

In response to a congressional inquiry, Deputy Secretary of State Richard Armitage issued a report making the case for restoring commercial links. "Assuming the Turkish-Armenian border was reopened, one would expect a reduction in transportation costs to and from Armenia, an increase in Turkish-Armenian trade and an improved overall economic environment in Armenia and eastern Turkey. Opening the border would result in an uninterrupted railroad link between Istanbul and Baku and the Mediterranean and Caspian Seas."[13]

The Turkish-Armenian Business Development Council (TABDC) believes that reopening the Gyumri border gate would generate $300 million in trade during the first year. It also claims that opening the Armenian-Azerbaijani border would boost Turkey's trade with Central Asia cutting transportation costs by 35 percent. Armenia's exports would double in the short term and its gross domestic product, which currently stands at about $2 billion, would increase by an estimated 30 to 40 percent. Kaan Soyak maintains, "There is no obstacle for Turks and Armenians to start talking and collaborating. The closed border is the only barrier preventing intensified business and human relations. A closed border separating us makes no sense."[14]

When Prime Minister Recep Tayyip Erdogan visited Kars in May 2003, the mayor and chamber of commerce pleaded with him to open the border. TARC also arranged appeals by members of the U.S. Congress. Senator Mitch McConnell (R-KY) stated, "Opening the border [between Turkey and Armenia] is in America's national interest, as I believe it may help America in our war on terrorism."[15] Frank Pallone and Joe Knollenberg, cochairmen of the Congressional Caucus on Armenian Issues, wrote Powell, "While Turkey is a valued ally of the United States, particularly in our

effort to eradicate terrorism, its behavior toward Armenia is unaccept-
able. The failure of Turkey to lift its blockade of Armenia and establish
diplomatic relations is extremely troubling."[16] The border opening was
raised by Powell during his visit to Ankara on April 2, 2003. Vice President Dick Cheney, Secretary of Defense Donald Rumsfeld, and National
Security Advisor Condoleeza Rice also discussed it with Foreign Minister Abdullah Gul during his trip to Washington, D.C., on July 21, 2003.

Prior to TARC's establishment, the Turkish and Armenian foreign ministers had not met in almost two years. A combination of TARC's efforts
and the new security situation after September 11 helped catalyze regular meetings between Turkish and Armenian officials.

In February 2002, Ismail Cem and Vartan Oskanian met at the World
Economic Forum in New York. In March, the Republic of Armenia opened
a liaison office in Istanbul to the Black Sea Economic Cooperation Council (BSEC). In April, the Turkish National Security Council conducted a
comprehensive review of Turkish policy toward Armenia. Gunduz and
Ozdem Sanberk were asked to participate. A few days later, the Armenian and Turkish foreign ministers had a face-to-face at the Reykjavik
NATO meeting. In June, 2002, Cem and Oskanian met at the BSEC in
Istanbul. The next spring, Oskanian and Gul conferred on the sidelines
of NATO's ministerial meeting in Madrid. NATO held its first military
exercises in Armenia and Turkey's "Istiklal Marsi" national anthem was
played to welcome Turkish soldiers. Turkey's President Sezer wrote President Kocharian congratulating him on his re-election; Gul and Oskanian met again during the UN General Assembly in September 2003. As
a result of their regular contacts, Oskanian and Gul developed a good
personal relationship and would regularly talk on the phone.

* * *

TARC was constantly affected by geopolitical events outside of its
control. Though TARC was launched with a plan, it was forced to adjust
its approach almost from day one. One of the important lessons from
TARC's experience is the need to adapt activities to their context. Though
it is hard to quantify the effect of Track Two, Oskanian acknowledged its
important role promoting rapprochement between the governments of
Turkey and Armenia. For example, Track Two helped create a climate
making possible a change in Turkey's stance on Armenia's membership
in the World Trade Organization, which paved the way for Armenia's accession in 2003.

Though it occurred in the shadow of terror attacks against the twin
towers, TARC's Istanbul meeting marked a watershed in its activities.
Media principles were adopted. Both Turkish and Armenian members endorsed policy recommendations, such as normalizing visa procedures and

opening the border. In what would prove to be a key step in addressing the genocide issue, TARC also invited experts from the International Center for Transitional Justice to conduct a seminar on legal issues at TARC's next meeting in New York.

Recognizing the far-reaching effect of September 11, TARC members issued a joint statement after the Istanbul meeting acknowledging their "shock and deep regret." TARC discussed the impact of these tragic events on world affairs and, in this light, reaffirmed its resolve to "enhance mutual understanding, overcome differences and encourage cooperation."[17]

Notes

1. Paul Wolfowitz, Turgut Ozal Lecture at the Washington Institute for Near East Policy, March 13, 2002.
2. *Mirror Spectator,* October 17, 2001.
3. *California Courier,* November 1, 2001.
4. Statement by Prime Minister Bulent Ecevit, January 19, 2002.
5. Statement by Foreign Minister Vartan Oskanian at the Black Sea Economic Cooperation Council, June 25, 2002.
6. Statement by Foreign Minister Vartan Oskanian at TESEV, June 26, 2002.
7. ANN Groong, October 17, 2001.
8. Statement by Foreign Minister Vartan Oskanian at TESEV, June 26, 2002.
9. Armenian Radio Hour of New Jersey, October 17, 2001.
10. Radio Free Europe, January 13, 2002.
11. Radio Free Europe, July 28, 1998.
12. Interview with the author, August 6, 2003.
13. 2003 State Department Report on Economic Impact of Turkish/Armenian Border Closure and on Diplomatic Contacts with Both Parties on This Issue.
14. *Turkish Daily News,* January 9, 2002.
15. Statement by Senator Mitch McConnell, June 13, 2002.
16. Letter from Rep. Frank Pallone and Rep. Joe Knollenberg to Secretary of State Colin Powell, December 3, 2001.
17. TARC Joint Statement, September 25, 2001.

9

RECONCILIATION DILEMMA

Theodore C. Sorensen had a calming effect on members of TARC. Sorensen is a vastly accomplished and venerable gentleman. He achieved national prominence as a speech writer and senior advisor to President John F. Kennedy. Among his many achievements in public service, Sorensen played a key role in helping to resolve the Cuban missile crisis. He is respected for his intelligence and political acuity; Sorensen is also known for his dry sense of humor and pithy truisms.

Sorensen is a board member of the International Center for Transitional Justice (ICTJ). The center was founded by Alex Boraine, the former deputy director of the South African Truth and Reconciliation Commission, to advise emerging democracies on addressing legacies of human rights abuse. Like Sorensen, Boraine exudes the wisdom born from experience. ICTJ also includes a first-rate team of experts on truth and reconciliation processes. Among them is Paul van Zyl, an erudite young lawyer who worked with Boraine in South Africa.

Gunduz Aktan called me from his Aegean island in July 2001. Insisting that legal action was the only way to confront the campaign for genocide recognition, he traveled to The Hague and interviewed experts at the International Court of Justice (ICJ). Gunduz wanted TARC to call on the governments of Turkey and Armenia to seek legal arbitration finally settling the genocide allegations. Gunduz asked me to find experts who could advise TARC.

In the late 1980s, I had participated in a congressional briefing on human rights in Guatemala. I remembered the solid contribution of Priscilla Hayner, a panelist who had talked about Guatemala's postwar truth and reconciliation process. I contacted a colleague at Human Rights Watch and learned that Hayner had joined ICTJ.

TARC's November 2001 meeting in New York got off to a smooth start. I had asked the Metropolitan Museum to open after-hours and arrange a special tour of its dazzling Mogul jewelry collection. At dinner, TARC members received an "I Love New York" T-shirt. There was good-natured joking as TARC members jostled for the right size.

Feelings of camaraderie were short-lived. Andranik Migranian accused Gunduz of violating the media principles we had agreed to at our last meeting; Gunduz accused Andranik of the same. Van Krikorian expressed his displeasure with Ozdem Sanberk, whose remarks had been used to discredit TARC. Back and forth we went with one accusation after another. TARC members aired their frustrations and vented hostilities.

After several hours of verbal sparring, I tried to refocus the group by going over our upcoming agenda. The ICTJ "Seminar on Legal Issues" would highlight international models for reconciliation. I highlighted some of the unique challenges facing TARC. Truth and reconciliation commissions (TRCs) are usually official bodies with a mandate to investigate historical events and recommend criminal prosecution. TARC has no such authority. The seminar was solely for information purposes and, like TARC, ICTJ has no official standing.

I picked up Ted Sorensen at his home the next morning. Sorensen had recently suffered a stroke, which impaired his eyesight and limited his mobility. His mind was still crystal clear and his tongue sharp as a whip. On his cane, Sorensen was an imposing figure. When we arrived at the seminar, the Turks and Armenians were on their best behavior. Sorensen's introductory remarks were sobering, serious, and hopeful. He reminded us that "We are not here to judge anyone. Justice is blind. Ill health took my sight several months ago, but it is coming back and I can see a future for your work."[1]

Transitional Justice

Sorensen explained ICTJ's approach to transitional justice.

> As political transition unfolds after a period of violence or repression, a society is often confronted with a difficult legacy of human rights abuse. In attempting to come to terms with past crimes, government officials and non-governmental advocates are likely to consider both judicial and non-judicial accountability mechanisms, and are increasingly employing a combination of both. Whether seeking to prosecute individual perpetrators, offer reparations to victims of state sponsored violence, convene a truth commission, implement institutional reforms or remove human rights abusers from positions of power, a society in

political transition often confronts extremely difficult challenges addressing its past.[2]

Models

Hayner provided an overview of transitional justice mechanisms and described different truth and reconciliation processes. Since 1973, more than twenty truth commissions have been established around the world. Most were created by governments and authorized by national parliaments. Some were established by international organizations such as the United Nations, and a few by NGOs.

She discussed the efficacy of a truth and reconciliation process in absolving the pain, injustice, and legacy of hatred. Hayner explained that TRCs are intended to unsilence the past by harmonizing the need of victims to remember with their desire to forget. Testimonies give voice to victims and have a healing effect on both the individual as well as society as a whole.[3]

The goal of a truth and reconciliation process is to build confidence among stakeholders in societies emerging from periods of repression. To end a cycle of violence, TRCs also seek to combat the culture of impunity by entrenching the rule of law. TRCs seek to prevent the recurrence of human rights abuses through recommendations institutionalizing reform, such as civilian control over the military or human rights training for police.

It is important that a clear mandate define the scope of TRC activities. For official bodies, the mandate may include the right to subpoena, seize evidence, and seek prosecution. TRCs consider events occurring over a specific period of time. They can focus on recent events, or they can go back decades or generations. For example, Australia's TRC covered many years, focusing on the "lost generation" of aborigines. The TRC usually exists for a prescribed period of time and typically produces a formal report at the end of its work. The TRC is a neutral enterprise established to forge consensus and document events.

Hayner compared the experience of TRCs in Chile, Guatemala, Argentina, El Salvador, and South Africa. The South African Truth and Reconciliation Commission is usually heralded as the most effective for promoting individual and national healing. Not only did it address prominent cases, such as those of Steve Biko and Winnie Mandela, it also documented everyday violence that touched the lives of South Africans.

She also described how public information campaigns inform stakeholders of the commission's purpose, tools, role, and limitations. Informing the public enables acceptance of political decisions governing the truth and reconciliation process. Every TRC faces an ethical dilemma. What is the best balance between amnesty and accountability?

Truth-telling

Truth is prerequisite to progress in any war-torn or traumatized society. Countries have addressed the need for documentation with different strategies. For example, Chile organized a "Historians' Manifesto;" Cambodia gathered testimony through the "Genocide Project;" Guatemala emphasized "historical clarification."

Narratives include individual testimonies, which enshrine events as insurance against denial or collective amnesia.[4] Truth-telling typically acknowledges individual suffering and has a healing effect on the teller. The process gets more complicated when suffering forges a collective conscience and group political identity. The concept of a "national victim" poses additional challenges to acknowledgment and contrition.

Martha Minow emphasizes the restorative power of truth-telling, which dignifies the victim and enables individual healing as the basis for reconciliation.[5] The Inter-American Commission on Human Rights describes the legal responsibility of governments to investigate and remedy human rights abuses under previous regimes. "Every society has the unalienable right to know the truth about past events, as well as the motives and circumstances in which aberrant crimes came to be committed, in order to prevent repetition."[6]

Violence tends to recur in societies where truth is obscured; Haiti's cycle of violence is exemplary. The Front for Advancement and Progress (FRAPH), a paramilitary group responsible for terror tactics during the rule of "Papa Doc" Duvalier, had links to the CIA. The U.S. took possession of 160,000 pages of documents, as well as incriminating photos and videos, before they could become part of the public record. Since amnesty was not offered in exchange for testimony, criminals had no incentive to testify. Many FRAPH members went into hiding or sought sanctuary in the United States. FRAPH's Emmanuel "Toto" Constant avoided prosecution by moving to Brooklyn; General Raoul Cedras was given political immunity and exiled to Panama. Some FRAPH members even found their way into Haiti's caretaker government after President Jean Bertrand Aristide was forced into exile in February 2004.

Getting to the truth is not always simple, especially when "multiple truths" exist. In conflict situations, all sides have their own version of the truth and are adamantly convinced they know what really happened. Uruguay implicitly recognized there are two sides to every story by mandating its TRC to consider guerilla crimes as well as those committed by the state.

Justice

The specter that amnesty means impunity hangs over most TRCs. Van Zyl explained that the truth and reconciliation process is not a substitute for accountability through trials. He emphasized that truth is complementary rather than a surrogate for justice. Van Zyl reviewed the evolution of international humanitarian law beginning with The Hague Convention (1907), the Nuremberg Tribunal Charter (1945), the United Nations Convention on the Prevention and Punishment of the Crime of Genocide (1948), and the four Geneva Conventions (1949). Together these treaties constitute the body of conventional and customary law defining state obligations to investigate and provide redress to victims of human rights abuse, mass violence, ethnic cleansing, or genocide.

A debate has raged between advocates of amnesty and those who demand accountability. Proponents of the former argue that amnesty avoids witch hunts and advances reconciliation. Others believe that reconciliation is delayed when justice is deferred. Without punishment for egregious crimes, there is no deterrent to prevent victimizers from committing crimes in the future. Unless individuals are held accountable, a tendency exists to hold the entire society or ethnic group responsible.

The debate played out in Yugoslavia. In 2000, President Vojislav Kostunica insisted that Slobodan Milosevic be tried by local courts staffed by judges left over from the Milosevic regime. Instead of prosecuting Milosevic for war crimes, Kostunica preferred a charge of corruption. This approach was rejected by Serbia's president Zoran Djindjic, who eventually arranged Milosevic's extradition to the International Criminal Tribunal for Yugoslavia in The Hague. The next year, assassins tied to Milosevic gunned down Djindjic in the streets of Belgrade.

Linking foreign aid with prosecutions is one way of encouraging accountability. For example, the U.S. conditioned its assistance to Yugoslavia with the extradition of Milosevic. Previously the U.S. linked the release of foreign aid to prosecutions in Chile, El Salvador, and Guatemala.

Reconciliation

Reconciliation does not occur through truth-telling alone. It is a more complicated and long-term process, which is both retrospective and prospective. John Paul Lederach believes that reconciliation "represents a place, the point of encounter where concerns about the past and future can meet. Reconciliation-as-encounter suggests that space for acknowledging of the past and envisioning of the future is the necessary ingredient for reframing the present. For this to happen, people must find ways to encounter themselves and their enemies, their hopes and fears."[7]

To "forgive and forget" is a utopian ideal. Reconciliation first requires acknowledgment. Contrition enables forgiveness by the victim. Choosing to forgive releases the individual from the need for payback. Reconciliation emphasizes healing at the expense of vengeance.

Reconciliation is also about relationships built on individual trust. It is advanced via the reform of institutions involved with past crimes, such as the military, the police, and the courts. While reconciliation is difficult enough between individuals, reconciling divided societies is even more challenging. Symbols are important to advance reconciliation. Using public areas to build memorials is symbolic. So is the inspirational conduct of individuals. Nelson Mandela emerged from twenty-six years in prison without malice. His forgiveness set an example for all South Africans—black, white, and Indian—to do the same.

When it comes to interstate reconciliation, postwar strategies should include the development of political, social, cultural, and economic relationships between nations with long-standing animosities. Interstate reconciliation may also be served through bilateral and multilateral structures enabling interaction and advancing shared interests. Cooperative linkages can begin informally and then become institutionalized over time. Friendship treaties and nonaggression pacts recognizing mutual sovereignty are also useful tools for reconciliation.

Real reconciliation demands that the voices of victims are heard and that their suffering is acknowledged. Unless there is accountability or transparency, victims will be condemned to a perpetual state of victimization. Without healing, they can become vulnerable to unscrupulous leaders who seek to exploit their anger and insecurity.[8]

Universal Jurisdiction

The October 1998 arrest of Augusto Pinochet in London at the request of a Spanish magistrate gave momentum to the notion of universal jurisdiction. The concept relates to the exercise of jurisdiction by national courts for crimes committed by non-nationals outside the territory of the state. Universal jurisdiction is a complement to evolving systems of international justice.

Established by the UN Security Council, the International Criminal Tribunal for Yugoslavia (1993) and the International Criminal Tribunal for Rwanda (1994) institutionalized the concept of extraterritorial justice. Expanding on the ad hoc tribunals, the Rome Statute established the International Criminal Court (ICC) in 1998. As an innovation in international justice, the ICC strengthens accountability and is a potential deterrent to future crimes.

By stipulating that the ICC only has jurisdiction when states are unwilling or unable to prosecute domestically, the Rome Statute underscores the principle of state responsibility. However, securing physical custody of defendants and arranging the cooperation of multiple states in investigations, apprehensions, and prosecutions limit the enforcement of extra-territorial justice. When effectively applied, the combination of universal jurisdiction and extra-territorial justice means that no one has immunity from prosecution unless amnesty is preferred over prosecution.

Amnesty

Archbishop Desmond Tutu defends the amnesty-for-truth compromise as a better option than the Nuremberg-type trials or a Chile-style blanket amnesty. In South Africa, Tutu maintains it was best that "Freedom was exchanged for truth."[9] As the vehicle for truth-telling, the South African Truth and Reconciliation Commission heard testimony from both victims and victimizers. It also considered abuses by both sides, including those who fought against apartheid, such as President Thabo Mbeki. Amnesty was awarded to those who confessed their crimes. In what became a heart-wrenching daily soap opera, the hearings were publicly broadcast and widely reported. The South African TRC enshrined the importance of amnesty. It was designed so that victimizers would have incentive to acknowledge and disclose their crimes. When perpetrators know they will be held legally accountable, it is difficult to secure detailed confessions that are essential to constructing a narrative of the truth.

In 1978, Chile's military regime declared a self-amnesty. El Salvador's TRC also ruled out military trials. Established by Raoul Alfonsin in 1983, Argentina's TRC was mandated to investigate disappearances that occurred during seven and a half years of military rule. Horrific stories were recounted of political prisoners tortured and tossed from airplanes. Though President Carlos Saul Menem pardoned officials convicted in closed-door trials, newly elected president Nestor Kirchner encouraged the Argentinean Senate to repeal controversial amnesty laws that prevented the prosecution of military officers accused of kidnapping, torture, and murder. Kirchner recognized that financial compensation was not enough for families of the victims.

The transition to democracy is often difficult and tumultuous. During the transition, outgoing military regimes may fear that democratic change will bring them to account for past human rights abuses. Newly elected civilian leaders in emerging democracies often choose to declare amnesty rather than pursue punitive measures that could derail progress. For example, Uruguay's new generation of pro-democracy leaders feared reprisals and ruled out trials.

Democracy

The truth and reconciliation commission is a useful tool for conflict transformation and postconflict peacebuilding. It is typically established by transitional governments as a way of consolidating political progress and democratic reform. Failure to address past violations undermines the rule of law and the legitimacy of new democratic institutions. As an alternative to prosecution, political leaders in emerging democracies may choose to issue an official apology or provide monetary or symbolic reparations to the victims and their families.

In many transitions, the perpetrators of past abuses continue to wield considerable power either in office or via proxies. They often work behind the scenes to protect themselves from retribution. Reform leaders must move quickly to strengthen institutions responsible for the rule of law. Enshrining human rights principles as official policy also helps guard against abuses. Many Eastern European countries went even further by adopting lustration laws that disqualified abusers from assuming positions of public trust.

Civil society also plays a key role. Postconflict peacebuilding can be enhanced through intergroup dialogues, which bring together stakeholders affected by the truth and reconciliation process. Highlighting the TRC's work also mobilizes the polity as watchdogs of reform and guardians of political progress.

Next Steps

ICTJ's "Seminar on Legal Issues" helped inform TARC's next steps. Sorensen was an able chairman and the ICTJ professionals were top-notch. TARC agreed to discuss ICTJ's future activities at its meeting the following day.

That evening Ahmet Ertegun hosted us for dinner at his elegant Manhattan townhouse. His residence is decorated with beautiful art and, in his private study, Ertegun has signed photos of rock stars such as Eric

Clapton. As chairman of Atlantic Records, Ertegun is an icon in the music and entertainment industry.

Ahmet Ertegun's father was Turkey's ambassador to Washington when Ahmet started collecting jazz. His interest in music was esoteric given his family's background in diplomacy. Ertegun's father negotiated the 1923 Lausanne Treaty that established the Republic of Turkey.

Helena Finn joined us for dinner. So did Kieran Prendergast, the UN Undersecretary General for Political Affairs, who served the British Foreign Office for many years in Turkey. To welcome his guests, Mr. Ertegun rose from the dinner table and, with enormous gravitas, implored the group, "Reconciliation is hard work. Whatever obstacles you face, do not give up."

* * *

Meeting with ICTJ the next day, Gunduz proposed that TARC request ICTJ conduct an analysis on the applicability of the Genocide Convention to the "so-called genocide" of Armenians. Van Krikorian and the Armenians were surprised. Though Gunduz wanted a strictly legal analysis, the term "applicability" could be interpreted in different ways.

The Turks and Armenians caucused in private rooms to discuss Gunduz's proposal. I shuttled back and forth answering questions, clarifying terms, and trying to bridge gaps. With the help of Van Zyl, we carefully negotiated the wording of ICTJ's mandate. When the language was finalized, the Turks and Armenians came together in the main conference room and agreed that "TARC requests that ICTJ facilitate the provision of an independent third party analysis of the applicability of the 1948 Genocide Convention to events at the beginning of the twentieth century [and that] this analysis would be made available to TARC on a confidential basis."[10]

Within minutes of adjourning, Andranik Migranian was on the phone with Radio Free Europe. Of all the Armenians, Andranik was the most outspoken with the media. Even though we agreed that the results of the analysis would be kept confidential, Andranik did not believe that confidentiality applied to the fact that such a study was to be conducted. To narrow possibilities for misrepresentation, I quickly issued a chairman's statement summarizing the agreement and sent it to TARC members.

Andranik's interview was in clear violation of the media principles and deeply upset the Turks. In a further violation of ground rules, Gunduz and Ozdem contacted ICTJ without telling me or their TARC colleagues. Ozdem's letter to Ted Sorensen read,

> I trust you are not aware of the row which emerged among Commission members on the interpretation of the clause in the draft statement regarding how to make public the outcome of the eventual study. The early leak of our

understanding to the press and the unfolding controversy has led us to think that until we overcome this hurdle would it not be wiser to refrain from studying the subject matter of our question as to whether the 1948 Convention would be applicable to 1915 events. It is our understanding that ICTJ was assigned to examine whether the Convention of 1948 could be applied retroactively to the events of 1915, not to examine whether the events of 1915 amounted to genocide in light of the Convention.[11]

At Gunduz's request, I involved ICTJ in the first place. If he was worried about their role, he should have raised his concern with me directly. Some TARC members made a habit of ignoring their commitments and undermining protocols critical to Track Two.

The Armenians were already besieged by a barrage of criticism. Had the visa regime for Armenian passport holders traveling to Turkey already been normalized, some pressures on TARC might have been relieved. In the Armenian Community, TARC supporters started to buckle. Even the Armenian Assembly had withdrawn its support.

When Sorensen gave me a copy of Ozdem's letter and asked how to proceed, I distributed it to all the TARC members. I learned that Ozdem had acted unilaterally without consulting TARC's Turkish members other than Gunduz. TARC's Armenian members issued a statement indicating,

Yesterday we were advised that the Turkish Commissioners unilaterally instructed the ICTJ to refrain from proceeding with the agreed upon study regarding the applicability of the 1948 Genocide Convention to the Armenian Genocide. Accordingly, the Armenian Commissioners regret to announce that we have notified Chairman David L. Phillips earlier today that the TARC is not going to proceed. We continue to believe that there is a need for full normalization of relations between Armenians and Turks and between Armenia and Turkey, contacts between members of the Armenian and Turkish civil societies, such as those which have been enabled through TARC, continue to be necessary to accomplish these goals.[12]

Support seemed to be crumbling all around. Steering his organization clear of controversy, Van Zyl wrote me that "ICTJ intends to suspend its work on commissioning an independent report until such time as both Turks and Armenians request us to proceed."[13] Though he had requested ICTJ's involvement in the first place, Gunduz wrote that ICTJ is "a center with no experience with genocide and with the Armenian question. It is not capable of doing a serious legal investigation."[14] My chairman's statement was merely intended to clarify the meeting's outcome, but Gunduz also attacked me for releasing the statement to TARC members "without authority or consent."[15]

Alex Arzoumanian believed that TARC's Turkish members had been pressured by officials in Ankara into withdrawing their consent for the genocide study. He said, "Mutual trust and respect for agreements is vital for the success of any joint undertaking and our commission in particular. Since these principles have been undermined, we Armenian members found it expedient to stop our participation for the time being."[16]

TARC's opponents were jubilant. The Armenian Revolutionary Federation (ARF) described the Armenians' statement as "belated recognition" of TARC's failure. The Armenian National Committee of America (ANCA) said the collapse of TARC "puts aside a barrier" to the genocide recognition campaign, and ARF reiterated its view that TARC was a Turkish ploy intended to derail international recognition of the Armenian genocide.[17] Headlines announced that TARC was dead.

Notes

1. Statement by Theodore C. Sorensen, New School University, November 21, 2001.
2. ICTJ Annual Report, 2002.
3. Priscilla B. Hayner, *Unspeakable Truths: Confronting State Terror and Atrocities,* Routledge, 2001.
4. Willie Henderson, "Metaphors, Narrative and 'Truth': South Africa's Truth and Reconciliation Commission," *African Affairs,* Vol. 99, No. 396, 2000.
5. Martha Minow, "Between Vengeance and Forgiveness: South Africa's Truth and Reconciliation Commission," *Negotiation Journal,* Vol. 145, October 1998.
6. Annual Report of the Inter-American Commission on Human Rights, 1985–86.
7. John Paul Lederach, *Building Peace: Sustainable Reconciliation in Divided Societies,* U.S. Institute of Peace Press, 1997.
8. Alex Boraine and Paul van Zyl, "Moving on Requires Looking Back," *International Herald Tribune,* August 1, 2003.
9. Desmond Tutu, "Reconciliation in Post-Apartheid South Africa: Experience of the Truth Commission," *The Art of Peace,* edited by Jeffrey Hopkins, 2000.
10. Chairman's statement, November 21, 2001.
11. Letter from Ozdem Sanberk to Theodore C. Sorensen, December 10, 2001.
12. Statement by TARC's Armenian members, December 11, 2001.
13. Letter from Paul van Zyl to the author, December 14, 2001.
14. *Radikal,* December 10, 2001.
15. Ibid.
16. Radio Free Europe, December 12, 2001.
17. Radio Free Europe, December 12, 2001.

10

TAKING STOCK

Both sides quickly came to regret TARC's demise. After Ozdem Sanberk's letter, I was in touch with the man in the fedora hat. Knowing Ozdem would not act without instructions, I insinuated that Ankara was responsible for scuttling the initiative. Just mentioning the Genocide Convention stirred anxiety in the Turkish Foreign Ministry.

I also reported the breakdown to U.S. officials whom I believed would relay concerns to their Turkish counterparts. In addition, I described events to several senior columnists in Istanbul, as well as other well-placed international journalists. My purpose was to bring the Turks back to the table. Their renewed commitment would stiffen the Armenians' backbone and provide impetus to get back on track.

Linking TARC's problems to officials in Ankara may have finally precipitated action on the visa regime. On January 10, 2002, the Turkish government changed its visa procedures for Armenian passport holders. The new policy came too late to save TARC but just in time to help resurrect it.

Ustun Erguder was designated by his Turkish colleagues as liaison. He wrote, "We consider the unfortunate discord to be a procedural dispute. It was never the intention of the Turkish group to renege on the commitment it had undertaken for a study by the ICTJ. It is still our view that TARC is a useful instrument of track two diplomacy to promote reconciliation and friendship between Turks and Armenians. We believe that under the present circumstances any future meeting, if it can be arranged, should be regarded as a salvage operation. The Turkish group is ready to undertake this effort."[1]

Ustun was deeply committed to reconciliation. He listened more than he talked and always showed respect to others. His dignified demeanor, innate intelligence, and earnest effort were real assets to TARC. Ustun insisted, "TARC can be salvaged."[2]

* * *

Van Krikorian received many supportive messages from Armenians around the world. It was ironic that Armenians would attack TARC in public but support it in private. Encouraged by widespread support, Alex Arzoumanian maintained that "TARC has not formally ceased to exist and may still resume its activities. We will discuss the situation and try to look for ways out of the situation together."[3]

After the dust settled, we began discreetly exploring ways to revive TARC. It was agreed that this time discussions would have to be strictly confidential. We learned from past experience that flying below the radar could help avoid pressures that accompany public expectation. Each side designated a coordinator to simplify communications; Van would represent the Armenians and Ilter Turkmen, the Turks.

The ICTJ analysis was essential. Unless TARC found a way to address the genocide, Van was convinced it should be disbanded. TARC originally emphasized small steps and practical areas for cooperation, which would build momentum toward tackling core issues. The intense pressure to deliver results had taken its toll.

Van and Ilter met at the penthouse restaurant in Rockefeller Center. In the past, it looked out on the city skyline where the World Trade Center once stood. Now there was just an empty space where the twin towers used to be. Lamenting TARC's difficulties, Ilter felt genuine remorse over the negative turn of events. Though they had jousted at previous meetings, Van and Ilter had developed professional respect and a personal liking. Their chemistry proved pivotal to sustaining the process. Van is a thoughtful lawyer whose analytic abilities are matched by strong strategic thinking. Ilter is also a strategic player. He personifies the elder statesman, exuding poise, professionalism, and experience.

The next day we drove to my country house in the Hudson River Valley of upstate New York. Built in 1732, the home sits on fifty acres of rolling hills. There's a sign on the red barn that reads, "Camp David." It is the perfect environment for a soul-searching retreat.

After lunch we went out for a walk in the woods. I let Van and Ilter go strolling by themselves. As they meandered, I reflected on my warm feelings for them. I had grown fond of both Van and Ilter. It gave me great pleasure to have my home used as a setting for their discussion.

Later we huddled around the fireplace. Van and Ilter regretted that some TARC members had created acrimony through their actions, comments, and writings. The resulting distrust had undermined TARC. We agreed that TARC, in its present form, could not continue.

Van maintained it would be impossible to gather the old group and simply pretend that nothing had happened. He wanted Gunduz Aktan and Ozdem to resign. The well had been poisoned. Distrust had become dislike.

Ilter resisted Van's request that we jettison Gunduz and Ozdem. Ilter insisted that he too would step down if his colleagues were asked to go. Though there was occasional friction between them, Ilter strongly defended Gunduz. Ilter is not one to embarrass or undermine a colleague.

Van had always said that there might only be one chance to get it right. Had TARC lost that chance? They considered discontinuing their efforts. Instead of giving up, they finally agreed that TARC should evolve into a new entity. To avoid wild speculation about its status or allegations of failure, there would be no public announcement. The reconciliation process would simply evolve into a new vehicle with Van and Ilter acting as coordinators during the transition.

I was keeping Ted Sorensen informed of developments. The International Center for Transitional Justice (ICTJ) insisted they would only facilitate a legal analysis if requested by Turks and Armenians. Their letter did not specify, however, which Turks and Armenians. My effort focused on preserving a core group, which could revitalize its collaboration with ICTJ.

Always irrepressible, Andranik Migranian publicly called for the removal of some Turkish TARC members as a precondition for proceeding. Ilter conferred with his colleagues and relayed a proposal to Van. The Turkish Foreign Ministry wanted Gunduz to stay involved; Gunduz would only step down if Andranik did as well. Van rejected the swap. If Andranik's dismissal was the price for getting rid of Gunduz, then TARC would have to live with them both.

Van met with TARC's Armenian members in Yerevan and they agreed to go forward. I traveled to Istanbul to brief the Turkish side. Everyone showed up except Gunduz. Emboldened by his support from Turkey's establishment, Gunduz was becoming increasingly obstructionist in exercising a veto over the group. Ustun would later lament, "We made a mistake letting Gunduz be the only one to contact the Foreign Ministry."[4]

At our meeting, Turkish TARC members agreed to go forward with ICTJ. But after conferring with Gunduz, Ilter called to say they were not able to reach consensus and could not proceed. The Turks insisted on a strictly legal analysis. They were concerned that the study would also consider "legislative intent"—motivation by the drafters to apply the spirit of the Convention to events that occurred prior to the treaty coming into force. I urged Ilter to clarify his concerns directly with ICTJ.

On March 26, 2002, Van, Ilter, and Ustun dined at Bruno's and discussed procedures for the next day. At my New York apartment the following morning, Sorensen and Alex Boraine met privately with Van and then Ilter. Ustun also joined the discussion with Ilter and then we all met together. The purpose of the meeting was to discuss recent developments and explore strategies for managing the process. Both Van and Ilter emphasized their "red lines."

* * *

Efforts to revive TARC were a poorly kept secret. Radio Free Europe reported, "Members of TARC are maintaining unofficial contacts in a last-ditch effort to salvage the U.S.-backed initiative."[5] AZG announced that "TARC is restarting its activity" under a new name and with different members.[6] "TARC did not fold," asserted the Armenia News Network.[7] Suspecting that TARC was trying to revive the ICTJ analysis, Dashnaks charged Sorensen with bias. They cited his membership on the board of the Central Asian American Enterprise Fund, which was chaired by Stephen Solarz, the self-declared "Congressman from Istanbul."

To calm speculations, I went to Yerevan for meetings with Vartan Oskanian and other key figures. Andranik announced my arrival: "Phillips is holding consultations with Armenian and Turkish participants in an attempt to salvage the initiative. The outcome of those contacts will determine when, under which format and with whose participation the commission will resume its work."[8]

TARC was accused of not being inclusive. So I made a point of meeting with its critics in the Dashnak Party, the People's Party, the National Democratic Union, and the National Unity Party. At a dinner hosted by Ambassador John Ordway, they indicated that enlarging TARC's membership would make it more acceptable. However, their visceral hatred of Turks made it hard to envision them as members of TARC.

At a press conference on April 22, I confronted the reporter from *Yerkir,* ARF's official publication. I deliberately chastised him for irresponsible journalism and spreading disinformation. The next day *Yerkir* printed a photo of me on the front page with the headline "Enemy of the Armenian Nation Visits Yerevan." Soon thereafter, the European Armenian Federation announced that thirty-three groups had joined more than one hundred organizations in Greece, France, Italy, and Germany to condemn TARC.

Gunduz stirred more rancor when he wrote on May 22, "The Armenians were the losing party. That is why their losses in terms of life, property, and 'lands' are much greater than ours. As the winning party, the Turks must understand and show magnanimity for the suffering of the Armenians. There will always be an Armenian minority within us and an Armenia at our borders." Undermining TARC's efforts, Gunduz proposed a series of commissions: a Demography Commission to calculate the Armenian population; an Archive Commission to study documents; a History Commission to develop the facts; and an Arbitration Commission to determine if the events constitute genocide. He added, "Once the question of genocide is removed, it will be easier to further the reconciliation process."[9]

* * *

As stipulated in the original terms of reference, Van and Ilter agreed that TARC should meet to review its first year's activities. The meeting would also clarify TARC's support for the ICTJ analysis and determine the ongoing viability of the commission. If TARC agreed to fold, I planned to write a report and release it to the public.

To prepare for TARC's review meeting, I organized a conference call with Van, Ilter, and ICTJ. Sorensen was keen to go forward, but Boraine was wary. ICTJ maintained its position that the legal analysis must be requested in writing by both sides.

In July 2002 the review meeting was held in Bodrum, a seaside resort near the summer homes of several TARC members. I carried a letter from Sorensen outlining the terms of ICTJ's participation. Upon receiving authorization from TARC, I would act as ICTJ's "client." ICTJ would facilitate the analysis after consulting with Van and Ilter on their red lines. Once the study was complete, Van, Ilter, and I would be briefed orally and the study would be immediately released.

The pleasant surroundings of the Marmara Hotel had a positive effect. Everyone was relaxed and in shirt sleeves. Accompanied by his wife, Gunduz was gracious and gentlemanly.

TARC reviewed its goals to raise awareness, stimulate people-to-people contact, define policy objectives, and address core issues. Via its announcement, TARC had succeeded in calling attention to the need for Turkish-Armenian reconciliation. Prior to TARC, Armenian issues were virtually taboo in Turkey. TARC helped break the ice and a plethora of civil society initiatives ensued. American University's Track Two program helped build momentum by providing a ready source of project finance and technical assistance.

On matters of policy, Turks thought normalizing the visa regime was a major achievement. TARC's Armenian members downplayed it. They said the new procedure merely restored what existed previously. Despite repeated efforts, TARC failed to establish a policy working group. Instead of being in the vanguard ahead of governments, TARC had hidden behind them.

Other factors limited TARC's effectiveness. A gap in expectations existed between Turkish and Armenian members. Armenians pushed to achieve results; Turks preferred a slower process. There were more problems in between meetings than at meetings themselves. The gap dissipated momentum, and the absence of a secretariat limited follow-up.

Documenting discussions was also a hindrance. Negotiating the text of joint statements or chairman's statements caused controversy. Some TARC members also tended to act like officials rather than civil society representatives. Adhering to state positions limited creative interaction and stifled productive activity. Statements to the press and breaches in confidentiality eroded goodwill and became a flashpoint for problems.

As criticism intensified, TARC's inability to address the genocide issue raised doubts about the usefulness of continuing the process. We reviewed the history of ICTJ's involvement, including Gunduz's original request for legal advice. Even though the ICTJ analysis was nonbinding, it would be dangerous if one side won. TARC reaffirmed the importance of addressing core issues and, noting that the ICTJ study is something only Track Two could do, discussed procedures for reengaging ICTJ.

The Bodrum meeting was TARC's most successful. TARC decided to continue its work by setting up a group to work on policy recommendations. In addition to endorsing the resumption of rail service between Turkey and Armenia, TARC members proposed the establishment of trade development offices in Kars and Gyumri. The Turks offered to host a future meeting in Ankara, during which TARC would meet Turkish officials. TARC would also sponsor a "civil society summit" bringing together NGOs working on Turkish-Armenian cooperation.

We also negotiated a memorandum of understanding describing arrangements with ICTJ. TARC accepted Sorensen's letter. The memo also stipulated that ICTJ should meet with TARC members during the course of conducting its inquiry. After the presentation by a Turkish and an Armenian representative, each side would have the right to respond. Legal advisors could participate.

I was designated to negotiate the final terms of the memorandum. The Armenians had only one condition. They insisted that Gunduz present the case on behalf of the Turkish side. He asked me, "Why, do they think I'm red meat?"[11]

The memorandum spelled out technical procedures and finalized arrangements with ICTJ. It stated, "TARC irrevocably agrees that ICTJ should finalize the analysis and neither TARC nor any of its members may withdraw its support for said analysis for any reason at any time."[10] We agreed to keep arrangements confidential. TARC's joint statement indicated, "The review of year one activities was not complete so we are continuing to review our work."[12]

* * *

On September 10, Sorensen and Boraine, with their staff, met Van and Gunduz. Lawyers who do work for the Turkish embassy also participated. Gunduz believed that the study was already done and the hearing was just for show. To address his concern, Sorensen asserted, "So far the study is just a gleam in the eye. There are no conclusions and there is nothing on paper."[13]

Gunduz used a written statement for his intervention. He affirmed that the ICTJ study was not legally binding on Turkey or Armenia. As a strictly legal analysis, he believed the study should confine itself to whether the Convention applies retroactively. As a bedrock legal principle, he invoked Article 28 of the Vienna Convention on the Law of Treaties, "Nullum crimen sine lege"—penal sanction can only be based on existing law. Since treaties can only be applied retroactively if both sides agree, he proposed that ICTJ recommend that the Turkish and Armenian governments seek arbitration at the International Court of Justice in The Hague.

Gunduz argued that the killings of Armenians do not constitute genocide because the Armenians in the Ottoman Empire made up a political group fighting for national independence. He referred to Champtelier de Ribes, the French prosecutor during the Nuremberg trials, who articulated the uniqueness of the crime of genocide based on acts committed by the German government. "The defendant's crimes were so monstrous, so undreamt of in history through the Christian era up to the birth of Hitlerism that the term genocide had to be coined to define it." Gunduz also quoted Rafael Lemkin's magnum opus, *Axis Rule in Occupied Europe*. "Germany's practices actually provided the basis for developing the concept of genocide. German atrocities were so barbarous that genocide was coined as a term which could apply only to them."[14] Gunduz pointed out that Lemkin refers to Armenian massacres in footnotes along with the fall of Carthage, Titus's destruction of Jerusalem, and the wars of Genghis Khan and Tamerlane.[15]

Van also came to the meeting well prepared. He reminded ICTJ that the purpose of the exercise was to advance reconciliation and that the study should give both sides something. The ICTJ was asked not "whether the Genocide Convention applies" but to consider "the applicability of the Genocide Convention."

Van examined the criteria, definitions, and intent of the Convention's drafters. He distributed a copy of Lemkin's working notes, which stated, "Obtaining ratification by Turkey among the first twenty founding nations would be atonement for the genocide of Armenians."[16] Then Van conducted a textual analysis and reviewed subsequent legal and scholarly interpretations of the Convention. He also arranged for Samantha Power, director of Harvard University's Carr Center for Human Rights and a Pulitzer Prize winner, to join us on the phone.

Returning to the theme of reconciliation, Van insisted that the dispute was not between Turks and Armenians but between Turkish deniers and the rest of the world. He maintained that denial limits worldwide recognition of many righteous Turks who saved their Armenian neighbors. Van insisted that "We want ICTJ to state the obvious. Applicability of the Convention to the Armenian experience is a definitional example of genocide."[17]

ICTJ appreciated the great difficulty of its task. Boraine sent me a letter stating, "ICTJ has agreed to facilitate the provision of a legal analysis. The analysis will be performed entirely independently of the ICTJ. The analysis will not be conducted by any ICTJ staff member; nor will the ICTJ be involved in any way in seeking to influence the conclusions reached by the analysis. Our role is merely that of helping to identify an appropriate expert to undertake the analysis requested by TARC."[18]

Sorensen was adamant about limiting my participation in ICTJ's work. Expecting that the ICTJ study would serve as the basis for future activities he wanted to preserve my integrity as chairman of TARC.

Notes

1. Correspondence from Ustun Erguder to the author, December 20, 2001.
2. Radio Free Europe, January 17, 2002.
3. Radio Free Europe, December 12, 2001.
4. Interview with the author, August 6, 2003.
5. Radio Free Europe, March 8, 2002.
6. AZG, March 20, 2002.
7. Armenia News Network, March 20, 2002.
8. Mediamax, April 22, 2002.
9. Gunduz Aktan, "Solution of the Genocide Problem," *Turkish Daily News*, May 21, 2002.
10. TARC Memorandum of Understanding, July 12, 2002.
11. Discussion between Gunduz Aktan and the author in Bodrum, Turkey on July 12, 2002.
12. TARC Joint Statement, July 12, 2002.
13. Meeting notes, September 10, 2002.
14. "Genocide as a Crime Under International Law," *American Journal of International Law,* 1947, Vol. 41, No. 1, p. 149.
15. Statement by Gunduz Aktan, September 10, 2002.
16. New York Public Library, private collection of Lemkin's papers.
17. Statement by Van Krikorian, September 10, 2002.
18. Letter from Alex Boraine to the author, September 16, 2002.

11

APPLICABILITY OF THE GENOCIDE CONVENTION

Gunduz Aktan was nervous after his presentation to the International Center for Transitional Justice (ICTJ). He wanted me to evaluate his performance. I told him that his presentation was carefully prepared and "well lawyered." Gunduz still thought that the legal memorandum had been completed and that the whole process was just for show. I gave him my word that it was not. I reminded him of ICTJ's impeccable credentials and promised him that Ted Sorensen would ensure a balanced outcome. Gunduz indicated that balance was what he feared most. Gunduz called Van Krikorian before leaving New York. Their conversation further fueled Gunduz's concerns. Van was confident that the term "applicability" would be broadly interpreted.

As soon as he returned to Ankara, Gunduz fired off a message to TARC's Turkish members accusing Ilter Turkmen of condoning the concept of legislative intent in his meetings with ICTJ. He identified Van as his source. Gunduz is a seasoned bureaucratic infighter. He sensed that the analysis might not be entirely to his liking and was covering himself by assigning blame to Ilter. Van insisted that he said no such thing. I confirmed it; Ilter never had a word with ICTJ out of my earshot.

Gunduz is most animated on the attack. In addition to his constant rancoring of the Armenians, he unfairly impugned my impartiality in his column. When we first met with ICTJ, he told me he would "destroy them"[1] with his legal arguments. Now Gunduz had turned on me, as well as his fellow Turks. In the early stages, Gunduz's involvement was needed to establish TARC's credibility in establishment circles. His conduct was increasingly a liability.

Without Ilter, TARC would have collapsed and Ankara would have been blamed. Through his actions, Ilter proved it is possible to be both a gentleman and a patriot. Offended by Gunduz's baseless allegation, Ilter threatened to resign. TARC members implored him to stay involved.

Sorensen had promised that the ICTJ analysis would be accomplished within a month. However, the task proved more complicated than expected. The longer TARC waited for ICTJ to finish its work, the more nervous participants became. Ozdem Sanberk and Ustun sent anxious messages asking for a copy of the paper. I replied, "I have not seen the ICTJ study nor been informed of its contents. The whole point is to show it to Van on behalf of the Armenians and one of the Turkish members of TARC prior to its release."[2] Alex Boraine confirmed that the delay was due to the "thoroughness of research and the seriousness of its work."[3]

The Bodrum memorandum established procedures for finalizing the paper. It stipulated that ICTJ's draft would be shown to Van and Ilter prior to its release. After Gunduz's attack, Ilter refused the responsibility of reviewing the draft. So did Ustun and Ozdem. No one wanted to take the risk and be personally blamed. To overcome the procedural impasse, I invited all TARC members to New York at the end of January. The meeting was canceled at the last minute when Gunduz and Ilter ended up in the hospital and Ozdem's mother became ill.

TARC's Turkish members hoped that by indefinitely postponing the outcome they could put an end to the process. I was determined to find an alternative and arranged for Van and me to visit Istanbul. The analysis would be sent to Ilter prior to our arrival. He could share it with other TARC members and send comments to ICTJ. On February 4, 2003, we met to assess the paper and discuss next steps.

* * *

In its preamble, the analysis spelled out that it was a legal, not a factual or historical analysis. It was drafted by ICTJ's independent counsel based on the request to ICTJ in TARC's Memorandum of Understanding dated July 12, 2002. Findings were based on research, as well as the presentations by TARC members. As requested, the study provided an objective independent legal analysis regarding the applicability of the United Nations Convention on the Prevention and Punishment of Genocide to events that occurred during the early twentieth century.

The executive summary of legal conclusions indicated that

> International law generally prohibits the retroactive application of treaties unless a different intention appears from the treaty or is otherwise established. The Genocide Convention contains no provision mandating its retroactive application. To the contrary, the text strongly suggests that it was intended to impose prospective obligations only on the states party to it. Therefore, no

legal financial or territorial claim arising out of the Events could successfully be made against any individual or state under the Convention."

It concluded that

The term genocide, as used in the Convention to describe the international crime of that name, may be applied, however, to many and varied events that occurred prior to the entry into force of the Convention. References to genocide as historical fact are contained in the text of the Convention and its *travaux preparatoires.*

As it has been developed by the International Criminal Court (whose statute adopts the Convention's definition of genocide), the crime of genocide has four elements: (i) The perpetrator killed one or more persons; (ii) such person or persons belonged to a particular national, racial or religious group; (iii) the perpetrator intended to destroy in whole or in part that group, as such; and (iv) the conduct took place in the context of a manifest pattern of similar conduct directed against the group or was conduct that could itself effect such destruction.

There are many accounts of the Events, and significant disagreement among them on many issues of fact. Notwithstanding these disagreements, the core facts common to all various accounts we reviewed establish that three of the elements listed above were met: (1) one or more persons were killed; (2) such persons belonged to a particular national, ethnical, racial or religious group; and (3) the conduct took place in the context of a manifest pattern of similar conduct directed against the group. For purposes of assessing whether the Events, viewed collectively, constituted genocide, the only relevant area of disagreement is on whether the Events were perpetrated with the intent to destroy in whole, or in part, a national, ethnical, racial or religious group, as such. While this legal memorandum is not intended to definitively resolve particular factual disputes, we believe that the most reasonable conclusion to draw from the various accounts of the Events is that at least some of the perpetrators knew that the consequence of their actions would be the destruction, in whole or in part, of the Armenians of eastern Anatolia, as such, or acted purposefully towards this goal, and therefore, possessed the requisite genocidal intent. Because the other three elements identified above have been definitively established, the Events, viewed collectively, can thus be said to include all the elements of the crime of genocide as defined in the Convention, and legal scholars as well as historians, politicians, journalists and other people would be justified in continuing to so describe them.[4]

After a year of wrangling, the ICTJ memorandum was finally complete. Without the leadership of Ted Sorensen, the even-handedness of Alex Boraine, and the tireless work of Paul van Zyl, the ICTJ-facilitated analysis would not have been possible.

* * *

The Turks welcomed ICTJ's finding that the Convention could not be applied retroactively, thereby obviating any territorial or financial claims under the Convention. However, they claimed that ICTJ had exceeded its mandate in determining that the Events constituted genocide as defined by the treaty. The Armenians were generally pleased with the outcome. Though they publicly protested the finding on retroactivity, they knew all along that the treaty could not be applied retroactively.

For the most part, the ICTJ analysis was well received in Armenian circles. Emil Danielyan reported in Radio Free Europe, "The study concludes that killings of Armenians in 1915 constituted genocide. [It] deals a serious blow to the long-running Turkish policy of denial and could mark another milestone in international recognition of the tragedy."[5] The widely read *Haykakan Zhamanak* daily published an Armenian-language translation of the ICTJ analysis with photos of the Armenian members.[6] Former National Security Minister Simoniants offered additional accolades to TARC. "It is hard enough working with Turks. Imagine how difficult it must have been without support from fellow Armenians."[7]

The response was mild compared with the frenzy following TARC's creation. The ICTJ analysis was a serious piece of work spanning eighteen pages and including voluminous footnotes. It took time for people to study it and digest both the legal and political implications. Vartan Oskanian and others were wary of commenting publicly. Before being associated with the result, they waited to see which way the wind would blow.

In a private conversation with Van, Oskanian "offered congratulations" and said it was a great accomplishment.[8] However, he refused to publicly embrace the ICTJ analysis. Oskanian had his eye on Armenia's presidential elections. He was most concerned about the ICTJ finding on retroactivity. Relinquishing legal consequences would not sit well with Robert Kocharian's hard-line Diaspora supporters; Rouben Shugarian assured Oskanian that other international legal instruments could be used to claim liability, including civil actions and insurance claims.

Not all reports were positive. Having been caught in TARC's maelstrom, the Armenian Assembly of America only issued a cautious endorsement. The Dashnak Party rejected the study's finding that the Genocide Convention could not be used to claim territory or financial reparations. *Yerkir* indicated that the study merely acknowledged what was known all along.[9] The Dashnaks even hired their own legal consultant to counter ICTJ's finding on retroactivity.

* * *

The paper received surprisingly little attention in Turkey. It was released during a snowstorm over the week-long Bayram holiday. Moreover, Turkey was preoccupied with Iraq. Colin Powell had just given his report on weapons of mass destruction to the UN Security Council. The

Bush administration was clearly losing patience with the UN weapons inspections process and war was looking more likely.

TARC's Turkish members would later reflect favorably on the paper. Ustun indicated that the ICTJ paper "was excellent for Turkish purposes." Focusing on ICTJ's finding that the Genocide Convention cannot be applied retroactively, Ustun believed the paper "gets Turkey off the hook. It gives us an excellent way out. The glass is half full for both sides." He added, "It was not all we wanted, but there is enough for us."[10]

While others attacked, Gunduz was strangely silent. Professor Justin McCarthy, an adviser to the government of Turkey and a professor from Louisville University, wrote, "By the UN definition there was indeed genocide of the Armenians. There was also a genocide of the Muslims and of the Turks. The UN definition of genocide is essentially meaningless. It can be applied to almost any conflict." McCarthy expressed concern that the ICTJ analysis will reinforce prejudices against Turks. "Once the word genocide is used, people do not think of the UN definition. They think of what Hitler did to the Jews. [People] will blame the Turks without knowing anything of the real history." Regarding ICTJ, "Perhaps their good will was wrongly assumed. More likely they simply did not know what they were doing. TARC made a false step in asking the ICTJ for this opinion. I have never agreed with submitting historical questions to lawyers for final answers. What is needed is a commission of historians, not a commission of lawyers."[11]

Gunduz finally took aim. "The ICTJ was only asked to determine if the UN Convention on genocide was retroactively applicable for the 1915 events. ICTJ was not asked whether the 1915 events constituted an act of genocide." He welcomed ICTJ's finding that the Convention could not be applied retroactively, but blasted ICTJ for exceeding "the limits of its mandate."[12]

Van wanted to make sure that the right message was conveyed from the ICTJ paper. I distributed copies to contacts in the U.S. government, other governments, parliaments, media, and NGO representatives. TARC's nondescript cover note read, "The Turkish Armenian Reconciliation Commission (TARC) requested that the International Center for Transitional Justice (ICTJ) facilitate an independent legal analysis on the applicability of the 1948 Genocide Convention to events which occurred during the early twentieth century. On February 4, 2003, ICTJ provided the analysis on the subject. TARC members are evaluating the analysis and will meet to discuss it. In this context, TARC will explore future steps advancing the goal of reconciliation."[13]

* * *

TARC's next meeting was hosted by the Royal United Services Institute, a think tank associated with the British Ministry of Defence. On March 9, Sorensen and I flew to London. We anticipated heated debate. Sorensen started the session by describing his involvement negotiating Democratic Party convention platforms. Drawing comparison, he pointed out, "The ICTJ paper gives neither side everything, but each side something."[14]

Both Turkish and Armenian members of TARC expressed dissatisfaction. However, Gunduz was the only one to publicly distance himself from ICTJ's findings. Gunduz complained to Sorensen, "We were expecting a strictly legal analysis."[15] Alex Arzoumanian reassured him that Turkey's preoccupation with Iraq would make it easier for Gunduz to "escape criticism."[16]

We never intended to dwell on the ICTJ analysis. Since the genocide issue cast a shadow over every discussion, we needed to find a creative way to address it. I hoped its Solomonic approach would clear some space for more constructive interaction. With the ICTJ analysis behind it, TARC was ready for a new incarnation. Gunduz, Ozdem, and Sadi Erguvenc would step down after the London meeting. New Turks joined and TARC would continue its activities for another year.

At the London meeting in March 2003, TARC discussed how the recent elections in Turkey and Armenia would impact future work. David Hovhanissian described huge protests following Armenia's presidential elections on February 19. Armenians were outraged at Kocharian for stealing the election from Stepan Demirchian. Tens of thousands took to the streets demanding a second round. Election monitors from the Organization for Security and Cooperation in Europe issued a report citing serious ballot irregularities. Armenia's elections were far from "free and fair."

Even before the massacre of the Armenian prime minister and a number of parliamentarians in October 1999, politics in Armenia had been marred by corruption and violence. Stepan's father, Karen Demirchian, was speaker of the parliament during the attack. He died in a hail of bullets. Stepan accused the authorities of obstructing the assassination inquiry. Some commentators implicate Kocharian in the incident.

The Kocharian administration has ties to a cleptocracy, which has enriched itself at the expense of average Armenians. Corruption is rampant. The economy is depressed, and unemployment is widespread. Civil liberties have also suffered under Kocharian. For example, Kocharian stifled dissent by closing A-1 Television, the leading independent media outlet. Free speech advocates were beaten and protesters violently disbursed.

Many Armenians welcomed Stepan Demirchian as an alternative to Kocharian's corrupt and ineffective rule. Born in 1959, Demirchian is a young technocrat whose People's Party of Armenia is committed to clean government, social welfare, and economic development. Stepan tapped into the discontent of Armenians and generated a groundswell of popular support by promising fairness and better living conditions. He partnered with Aram Sarkisian, whose brother was slain in the 1999 parliament attack. Stepan and Aram had endorsed TARC and supported Turkish-Armenian parliamentary exchanges.

Armenian columnists expressed regret over the election. They believed that Stepan and Aram would have resisted the influence of Dashnak extremists and taken steps to benefit Armenia by promoting better relations with Ankara. Armenia suffers in large part because its leadership lacks the vision and creativity to address the country's problems. Kocharian's critics accuse him of catering to narrow constituencies for the sole purpose of staying in power. They maintain that he is an impediment to progress and an obstacle to normalizing relations.

* * *

Stepan Demirchian's failure to assume the presidency occurred just as Turkey's politics were turned upside down by the overwhelming victory of Recep Tayyip Erdogan's Justice and Development Party (AKP) on November 3, 2002. With 34.2 percent of the votes in Turkey's parliamentary elections, AKP's crushing victory paved the way for single-party rule for the first time in fifteen years.

In what the Turkish newspaper, *Sabah,* called the "Great Purge," Turkey's political dinosaurs—Mesut Yilmaz of the Motherland Party, Tansu Ciller of the True Path Party, and Devlet Bahceli of the Nationalist Action Party—all announced their resignations. Bulent Ecevit's inefficient incumbent Democratic Left Party, which was neither democratic nor leftist, received only 1.2 percent of the vote.

AKP rose from the ashes of Necmetin Erbakan's Islamic Welfare Party. Erdogan was a disciple of Erbakan, who came to power when Erbakan appointed him chairman of the Welfare Party's Istanbul branch and endorsed his candidacy for mayor. Islamic politics is new in Turkey, and the goal of establishing an Islamic state is deeply threatening to the country's establishment. In 1923, Ataturk rejected Islam as the state religion and established a secular republic. He closed the Caliphate, secularized academic curricula, and replaced Arabic script with a Latin one. He also disbanded religious courts and gave women the right to vote. As the guardian of Ataturk's secular democracy, the army was troubled by Erbakan's visit to Libya and overtures to Iran. It shut down the Welfare Party and banned Erbakan from politics.

Unlike its predecessor, AKP learned to avoid language that would bring it into confrontation with secular institutions. Instead it opted for a popular message of democracy closer to the political center. Despite its

Islamic roots, AKP was careful to present itself as a modern, conservative party in the mold of Europe's Christian Democrats.

AKP was swept into power by a classic protest vote. Sabanci University's public opinion survey documented an increase in patriotism, xenophobia, and ethnic nationalism in Turkey. A majority of Turks was deeply dissatisfied with the government's management of the economy and angry over their diminished expectations.[17] AKP tapped into the alienation of many Turks. AKP also appealed to the conservative streak in Turkey's Muslim population by targeting politically popular issues such as regulations banning Turkish women from wearing headscarves in universities and state buildings.

Though he is AKP's undisputed leader, Erdogan was not able to run for parliament. During a campaign rally at the eastern Anatolian city of Siirt, Erdogan read a poem with Islamist overtones—"The mosques are our barracks, the domes our helmets, the minarets our bayonets and the faithful our soldiers."[18] While serving as Istanbul's mayor, he was convicted of inciting religious hatred and spent four months in jail. The Supreme Elections Board banned felons from standing for parliament. After taking control of the parliament in January 2003, AKP amended the constitution allowing Erdogan to run from Siirt in a by-election. Erdogan became prime minister in mid-March 2003.

Erdogan is fundamentally a champion of reform and social justice. Though he supports Turkey's Western-oriented foreign policy, hard-liners in the establishment were appalled by Erdogan's independent streak and specifically balked at his willingness to sacrifice Denktash in order to advance Turkey's case for membership in the EU. Under pressure from the National Security Council, Erdogan quickly backtracked. Deborah Sontag wrote, "[Erdogan] greatly disappointed those who thought he would be an agent of change. To take on the military too soon might be suicidal, but to defer confrontation could also render him impotent."[19] Instead of directly confronting Erdogan, establishment opponents sought other ways to weaken him. The National Security Council's manipulation of events in Iraq was motivated by a desire to undermine Erdogan as well as a genuine opposition to the war.

Ozdem told TARC's Armenian members that Turkey was much too distracted by Iraq and its domestic political drama to pay much attention to Armenian issues. Gunduz announced, "I cannot continue with TARC."[20] Ozdem insisted, "TARC needs new blood."[21] Others also wanted to resign.

At the London meeting, we set dates for a seminar at Harvard University and discussed traveling to Ankara for meetings with Turkish officials. I tried to organize these activities, but the Turks did not respond. I canvassed the group to determine which Turks were still with us. I wrote

TARC's Turkish members, "I gather from our discussions that some of you want to step down from TARC in order to enable new participants from Turkey to join. Though you will be missed, I understand the situation and am writing to discuss modalities for TARC's transition. TARC, as presently constituted, would have a final meeting in Turkey serving as its two-year review. Like you, I see value in an elegant TARC transition. It is important that we wrap up constructively."[22]

Van was hoping that the U.S. State Department would issue a statement supporting TARC and endorsing the ICTJ analysis. But the Bush administration was preoccupied with Iraq and engaged in negotiations to base U.S. troops in Turkey. The U.S. government's response to the ICTJ analysis was finally articulated by John Ordway. "I think that the report prepared by the International Center for Transitional Justice at the request of TARC was a very solid and strong contribution to the dialogue and discussion that has to take place between Turkey and Armenia and between Turks and Armenians."[23]

By the time Ordway issued his endorsement, the first phase of the war in Iraq was winding down. The U.S. and Turkey had a major falling out and relations were at a low point. Turkey's fall from favor revitalized congressional efforts to recognize the Armenian genocide. It also motivated the Bush administration to press for opening the Kars-Gyumri gate.

Notes

1. Conversation between Gunduz Aktan and the author in New York on November 20, 2001.
2. E-mail message to Ustun Erguder from the author, November 26, 2002.
3. Conversation between Alex Boraine, Ustun Erguder, and Van Krikorian, December 4, 2002.
4. Legal Analysis Prepared for the International Center for Transitional Justice, February 4, 2003.
5. Emil Danielyan, "International Study Affirms 1915 Armenian Genocide," *Armenia Liberty,* February 10, 2003.
6. *Haykakan Zhamanak,* February 11, 2003.
7. Armenian Radio Talk Show, February 11, 2003.
8. Conversation notes, February 11, 2003.
9. "Yes, but ...," *YERKIR,* February 12, 2003.
10. Interview with the author, August 6, 2003.
11. Justin McCarthy, *The Turkish Forum,* No. 10879.
12. Gunduz Aktan, *Turkish Daily News,* February 17, 2003.
13. TARC Statement, February 7, 2003.
14. Meeting notes, March 10, 2003.
15. Gunduz Aktan, London, March 10, 2003.
16. Meeting notes, March 10, 2003.
17. Sabanci University, Turkish Pre-Electoral Behavior Study, October 2002.

18. Deborah Sontag, "The Erdogan Experiment," *The New York Times Magazine,* May 11, 2003.
19. Ibid.
20. Gunduz Aktan, London, March 10, 2003.
21. Ozdem Sanberk, London, March 10, 2003.
22. E-mail from the author, April 15, 2003.
23. *Armenia Liberty,* April 25, 2003.

12

WAR IN IRAQ

The Iraq war profoundly affected the context in which Turks and Armenians were conducting their dialogue. It also influenced the Bush administration's approach to Turkey and its willingness to press Ankara on Armenian issues. With the Pentagon pressing for permission to transit U.S. forces through Turkey to northern Iraq, Turkish-Armenian issues disappeared off the priority list. When Ankara rebuked Washington and war proceeded without Turkey's involvement, angry administration officials were all too willing to bash Turkey and include Armenia among its grievances. Later, the pendulum would swing back the other way when Pentagon officials petitioned Turkey to deploy ten thousand peacekeepers, and as overall conditions deteriorated in Iraq.

During the run-up to war, Turkey's erratic approach was blamed on Recep Tayyip Erdogan, whose Justice and Development Party (AKP) had won a smashing electoral victory in February 2003. Neither Washington nor Turkey's establishment knew what to make of Erdogan's meteoric rise to power. Embarrassed by his parochial background and his wife's insistence on wearing a headscarf as a symbol of her Islamic faith, Turkey's elite was deeply suspicious about Erdogan's plans to establish an Islamic state. Erdogan pronounced, "Democracy is like a streetcar. When you come to your stop, you get off."[1] The office of prime minister was an unexpected stop in Erdogan's political career.

Erdogan's AKP came into power promising reform. Instead its first months were defined by uncertainty and missteps. Erdogan talked about a compromise on Cyprus, but backpedaled under pressure from the Turkish General Staff (TGS). Despite steps to abolish the death penalty and expand Kurdish cultural rights, the European Union refused to set a date for starting negotiations on Turkey's membership. It promised to review

Turkey's candidacy at the end of 2004. Ankara blamed the International Monetary Fund for Turkey's continuing economic woes. When Kurdish earthquake victims took to the streets to demand assistance, AKP apparatchiks confronted them with riot police. Most of all, AKP was ill prepared to deal with the imminent war in Iraq.

Turkey was always one of America's strongest and most reliable allies. During the Gulf War, President Turgut Ozal acted decisively to support the international coalition. When planning the Iraq war of 2003, the Bush administration took Turkey's support for granted. The war plan called for stretching Iraq's defenses through a two-pronged offensive with troops entering Iraq from Turkey in the north and Kuwait in the south. In the past, the U.S. and the TGS would simply agree and it would be done. As always, Washington expected Turkey's establishment to deliver.

However, AKP's sweeping electoral victory introduced a new variable into decision-making. The war in Iraq was profoundly unpopular with Turkish citizens. Many Turks believed that aggression against Iraq was unjustified and illegal. They were also concerned about the effect of war on Turkey's economy. Turkey paid a steep price for its participation in the Gulf War. It claimed that UN sanctions against Iraq cost it $40 billion in lost trade and revenue.

The situation in Iraqi Kurdistan was most deeply disturbing to Turkey's establishment. Facilitated by Operation Northern Watch, U.S. and British protection had enabled the emergence of a quasi-independent Kurdish state in northern Iraq. Ankara was concerned that its de facto independence would inspire Turkey's restive Kurdish minority to seek something similar. Though up to 20 million Kurds live in Turkey, Turkey did not even admit it had a distinct Kurdish population until the mid-1990s. Kurds were called "Mountain Turks." When I made my first trip to Diyarbakir, Turkey's largest Kurdish city in the southeast, a big banner flew over the main street, announcing, "Everyone is happy to be a Turk." Many Kurds are integrated throughout the country and enjoy the same opportunities as other Turkish citizens. As proof, Turks pointed out that Ozal himself was part Kurdish.

More than a lack of political and cultural rights, Kurds in southeastern Turkey suffered draconian security measures from the state of emergency in the 1990s. After Abdullah Ocalan's arrest, PKK remnants survived in mountain camps across the border. Every spring, Turkish armed forces would launch an offensive against Kurdish guerillas. To the dismay of Massoud Barzani, president of the Iraqi Kurdistan Democratic Party, Turkish troops set up permanent bases in northern Iraq. When I visited Barzani in July 2002, he was furious with Turkey. He threatened action if Ankara sought a "Cyprus solution" in Iraqi Kurdistan.

In November 2002, Paul Wolfowitz and Marc Grossman traveled to Ankara to discuss military cooperation. Undersecretary of Defense Douglas Feith was convinced that Ankara would comply with Washington's demands. Formerly a paid lobbyist for Turkey, Feith was confident that Ankara would do what it was told.

Even though Erdogan was banned from parliament, President Bush treated him like a head of state when he came to the White House in December 2002. During his meeting in the Oval Office with Bush's national security team, Erdogan argued against removing Saddam Hussein. He warned that a Shiite regime with strong ties to Iran would emerge. In the event of war, the Americans made the case for Turkey's participation. Erdogan was noncommittal. Indicating that no decision could be made without authorization by the parliament, Erdogan left the meeting convinced that the U.S. would not undertake military action without Turkey. To do so would be riskier, take longer, and result in more casualties.

Even though the UN weapons inspections failed to uncover weapons of mass destruction, it had become apparent that the Bush administration was committed to removing Saddam. Initial military plans had 92,000 American troops and support personnel transiting through Turkey. On February 24, 2003, Foreign Minister Yasar Yakis met with Colin Powell to discuss the terms of Turkey's participation. Yakis sought a staggering total of $92 billion—$1 billion for every thousand troops to set foot on Turkish soil.

The Bush administration was aghast. At best, it was prepared to provide $6 billion in aid, which could be leveraged into $24 billion in credits. Yakis's opening bid was over the top. Though administration officials appreciated Turkey's concern about instability in northern Iraq, they rejected Yakis's demand for Turkish control of northern Iraq after the overthrow of Saddam Hussein.

The AKP leadership was dissatisfied with Washington's vague assurances. In addition, Turks were annoyed by racist depictions in the American press. Satirizing Yakis's offer, cartoons in several periodicals portrayed Turks as carpet salesmen and bazaar hagglers. Ankara did not take kindly to trying to extort money in exchange for its loyalty. Turkey's deputy permanent representative to the UN went on television to announce, "We are not prostitutes."

Erdogan is a pragmatist and, in a phone conversation with Bush, pledged to support the basing of American troops. Claiming respect for Turkey's democracy, the generals kept a low profile while offering assurances to Washington. U.S. officials were confident that the Turkish Grand National Assembly (TGNA) would approve the measure when it voted on March 1. In a staggering setback to the Bush administration's war plans, the measure was defeated by three votes.

The Turkish business community was shaken. Within 48 hours, the Turkish stock market plunged 12.5 percent and the Turkish lira fell 5 percent on fears that Turkey would lose the $6 billion in aid from Washington. Turkish commentators speculated that the military was working behind the scenes to discredit Erdogan. Even though AKP held nearly two-thirds of the seats in parliament, many deputies did not show up and there were numerous defections. Erdogan blamed the U.S. for rushing the vote in parliament before he could gather enough support. He also claimed that the U.S. had alienated the Turkish public with statements describing their reluctance as a bargaining ploy for more economic aid.

The Bush administration was incredulous. Erdogan was either disingenuous in claiming support or simply not experienced enough to impose party discipline and deliver the votes. U.S. officials immediately started angling for a new vote in the TGNA. Again Erdogan was reluctant to betray his supporters and dragged his feet. By now he had won the Siirt by-election but had not yet taken his seat in parliament. He told the Bush administration that a new vote would have to wait until he was sworn in as prime minister. Both Erdogan and the TGS were in no rush. They were convinced that the Pentagon could not go to war without Turkey.

The Pentagon's war plan included a ground offensive from Turkey targeting Iraqi Republican Guard units in Mosul and Kirkuk. It also called for extensive sorties by U.S. warplanes from Incirlik, just minutes from the Iraqi border. Planes from U.S. aircraft carriers in the eastern Mediterranean would fly across Turkish airspace to hit targets in Iraq. Approval had been given for American engineers to refurbish port facilities where the Army's 4th Infantry Division would be off-loaded. Anticipating a new vote in the TGNA, the Pentagon decided to keep its ships off the Turkish coast. While the parliament pondered, twenty-four cargo ships carrying the 4th Infantry Division's vehicles, supplies, and equipment waited for permission to unload.

Though the Bush administration appeared outwardly confident, it was making alternate arrangements. If Turkey refused to grant basing rights, plans were being made to send the ships to Kuwait. Rerouting the 4th Infantry Division was a logistical nightmare. It would take at least a week to sail to the Persian Gulf. In addition, there was concern that the routing could interfere with the passage of other cargo ships through the Suez Canal and overwhelm port facilities in Kuwait, which were already hosting several Army and Marine divisions. If Turkey refused to open a land bridge, arrangements to airlift troops directly into northern Iraq were also under consideration.

Washington was appalled by Ankara's handling of the situation. In an interview about Turkey's decision, Senator Jay Rockefeller (D-WV), the ranking Democrat on the Intelligence Committee, indicated, "It stunned me. We spent fifty years defending them in NATO. Along comes this opportunity and by three votes they decline to allow us to come in through the north."[2] William Safire accused Turkey of betrayal.[3]

After weeks of waiting for the TGNA, the Pentagon finally redirected the 4th Infantry Division to Kuwait. Though there would be no northern front, General Tommy Franks insisted that the U.S. could still prosecute the war successfully. The Bush administration sought overflight rights from Ankara. Erdogan had by now run the constitutional gauntlet and was sworn in as prime minister. But once again, he indicated that the parliament's approval was needed. Adamantly opposed to war, Turkish leaders sought further assurances about postwar Iraq before allowing the use of Turkish airspace.

Through the "Ankara Process," U.S. officials met with Turkish counterparts and Iraqi Kurdish representatives from the KDP and the Patriotic Union of Kurdistan. The Kurds were incensed by the proposal that Turkish troops occupy a 20 km buffer zone in Iraqi Kurdistan. They were also concerned about Turkey's support for the Iraqi Turkmen Front (ITF). Though there may be as many as two million Turkmen in Iraq, most are dispersed across the country. The ITF is financed and directed by Ankara. Ignoring Kurdish protests, the U.S. promised Turkey its buffer zone and guaranteed it a meaningful role in determining Iraq's future governance.

On March 19, the TGNA finally voted to permit overflight by U.S. war planes. It was the last NATO country to do so. Washington thought the deal was done. But after the vote, the TGS demanded a written guarantee that Turkish troops would be allowed to occupy northern Iraq. Without it, the TGS insisted that American planes would be barred from Turkish airspace.

U.S. officials were incensed. Powell held an impromptu press conference and angrily condemned the Turkish position. A senior administration official who had been involved in negotiations with Ankara said, "It feels like the Turks have taken a hot poker and stuck it in my eye. Don't they watch CNN? Don't they know that the war has already started?"[4] The Turks retreated from their position two days later. But the damage to U.S.-Turkish relations was done.

In the few months since coming into power, the AKP had been sandbagged by the "deep state" burning Turkey's bridges to the U.S., the EU, and the Arab world. Even Turkey's old friends in the Bush administration were incensed. With former French president Valery Giscard d'Estaing declaring that Turkey's acceptance would mean the "end of Europe," the EU deferred a decision on starting membership negotiations until December 2004.[5] The Arab world was also suspicious of Turkey. Threats to occupy Mosul and Kirkuk revived Arab fears of Ottoman imperialism. Despite its mixed ethnicity, Mosul is an Arab city to the Arab world.

Ankara envisioned that seizing northern Iraq would give it control of the rich Kirkuk oil fields. It would also undermine Kurdish aspirations for nationhood and help protect the Iraqi Turkmen from domination by Kurds. The original military plan had Turkish troops following on the heels of the 4th Infantry Division. Without U.S. forces as a buffer, Pentagon officials warned Turkey against adventures in northern Iraq. If Turkey invaded, there was a real possibility that the U.S. and Turkey could end up in a military confrontation.

Failure to open the northern front had huge implications for the conduct of the war, as well as postwar planning. It forced the U.S. to focus its operations entirely on the south, stretching supply lines and making U.S. forces vulnerable to attack. After a week of racing across the desert, coalition forces stalled south of Najaf and questions were raised about the Pentagon's military planning.

The 4th Infantry Division never made it into the theater of combat while major military operations were under way. When the Iraqi Republican Guard's "ring of fire" around Baghdad collapsed, U.S. troops pressed their advantage and rushed to the capital. Too few boots on the ground limited the coalition's ability to control the ensuing looting and chaos. Had the 4th Infantry Division been in play, the coalition might have been able to control the situation and establish better security.

Under intense pressure, Turkey decided against sending its troops into northern Iraq. Instead it pursued more insidious strategies. In April 2003, a Turkish Red Crescent convoy was stopped at a checkpoint. Weapons and explosives were discovered in bags thought to contain humanitarian supplies. The humanitarian workers were actually Turkish Special Forces infiltrating northern Iraq to assist ITF militias. The U.S. deported twenty-three Turkish Special Forces to Turkey.

On July 4, American troops detained eleven Turkish Special Forces on the grounds that they were conspiring to assassinate elected Kurdish officials in northern Iraq. The suspected Turkish assassins were detained and taken to Baghdad for interrogation. Press reports of handcuffed and hooded Turkish troops riled public opinion, which was already upset about the war and Turkey's subsequent exclusion from postwar arrangements. Gunduz Aktan wrote, "Have Americans forgotten how they felt when they saw their diplomats, eyes bandaged, dragged out of the U.S. embassy in Tehran during Khomeini's revolution? Turks feel the same about the U.S. treatment of their soldiers. Like Americans, they too will not forget." Hilmi Ozkok, TGS chairman, maintained that the arrest was the "biggest crisis" ever between the two NATO allies. Hursit Tolon, a top general, called the incident "disgusting" and cancelled a trip to America.[6]

The detention of Turkish troops raised serious questions about the relationship between the two NATO allies. American flags were burned. Protesters gathered at the American embassy and a bomb exploded at the consulate in Istanbul. An editorial in *The Economist* warned that "The specter of Kurdish renaissance, courtesy of the Americans, is jangling Turkish nerves." It called U.S.-Turkish relations a "partnership at risk."[7]

I was told there was irrefutable evidence that Turkish Special Forces had plotted to assassinate the Kurdish governor of Kirkuk. This was no surprise. During my visit to Iraqi Kurdistan in July 2002, Kurdish intelligence agents had shown me a videotape of Turkey's senior official in Erbil paying a hit man to kill the leading independent Iraqi Turkmen politician. In Iraqi Kurdistan, Turkey had been involved in a pattern of infiltration and disruption for at least a year.

With deference to the long-standing special relationship, members of Congress had muted their criticism of Turkey during the run-up to war in Iraq. Legislators were angered by Ankara's lack of cooperation during the war and by the gloating of some Turks over America's difficulties during the postwar period. A decidedly anti-Turkish mood dominated the Congress, which launched several initiatives concerning the Armenian genocide. Senator Jon Ensign (R-TN) and Senator John Corzine (D-NJ) introduced Senate Resolution 307, which commemorated the fifteenth anniversary of America's signing of the UN Genocide Convention and specifically mentioned the Armenian genocide as an example of events the Convention intended to prevent. A similar bill was introduced in the House Judiciary Committee. H.R. 193 commemorated the Genocide Convention and mentioned the Jewish Holocaust as well as the Armenian, Cambodian, and Rwandan genocides.

Gunduz Aktan charged that the bills were "payback." He asked, "Do you think that the Congress would even be considering the measure if our parliament has allowed the U.S. to use Turkish soil as a springboard for a northern front into Iraq?"[8]

Notes

1. Sontag, "The Erdogan Experiment."
2. CNN Late Edition, March 2, 2003.
3. *Armenia Liberty,* April 2, 2003.
4. Anonymous, March 21, 2003.
5. *Armenia Weekly,* January 4–10, 2003.
6. Yigal Schleifer, "U.S. now seeks Turkish troops for north Iraq," *Post Gazette,* July 22, 2003.
7. "A Partnership at Risk," *The Economist,* July 12, 2003.
8. Gunduz Aktan, "So-Called Armenian Genocide on the U.S. Congress Agenda," *Radikal,* July 14, 2003.

13

AT THE BORDER

TARC had consistently maintained that opening the Turkish-Armenian border would advance the goal of reconciliation. TARC members were cautiously optimistic when the *Turkish Daily News* reported that Ankara had decided to open Turkey's border with Armenia. The question was not if the border would be opened but when. "Last month witnessed unprecedented statements by Turkish officials about a possible thaw in relations with Yerevan. For the first time in its ten year blockade of Armenia, Ankara has suggested that the border between the two countries could be opened."[1]

Ankara was partly motivated by a desire to get U.S.-Turkish relations back on track. After the July 4 debacle, both countries decided to ease tense relations and consider ways of restoring their special relationship. An official at the American embassy in Ankara affirmed, "We are trying to get beyond this to a place where we have better coordination in Iraq."[2] A joint fact-finding team was established to investigate the detention of Turkish troops accused of plotting the assassination of Kirkuk's governor. Its statement expressing regret over the "unfortunate" incident fell far short of the apology Turks wanted.

Abdullah Gul initiated a visit to Washington in late July 2003. Gul was received by Dick Cheney, Donald Rumsfeld, Paul Wolfowitz, Advisor Condoleeza Rice, and Colin Powell. In their joint press session after a working lunch, Powell indicated that "[We] appreciate the significant offers of assistance we have received from Turkey for reconstruction, humanitarian and other important efforts in Iraq, to help the Iraqi people rebuild their society from the devastation caused by Saddam Hussein."[3]

At every meeting, Gul was reminded that the issue of genocide recognition was not going away. He was told that real progress was the best way of deflecting pressure. Most important, administration officials emphasized that Turkey's national interests would be served by opening its border with Armenia. Normal travel and trade would stimulate Turkey's economy and enhance Ankara's standing in the region. Gul was reminded that Armenia represents an export market for Turkish products, including consumer goods, agricultural commodities, and equipment. Opening the border would catalyze commercial opportunities in the fields of energy, trade, and tourism valued at $1 billion per year. In addition, auto and rail links would position Turkey as the bridge between Europe and Asia. Restoring rail transport would enable regional energy projects, link regional power grids, and stimulate the economy through lower electricity costs. Goods shipped via Turkish ports would also generate significant transportation fees. The twenty-first-century "Silk Road" could become a windfall for Turkey.

Gul expressed concerns that opening the border would inspire territorial claims by Armenia; U.S. officials assured him that such concerns were ill founded. They pointed out that Armenia has never claimed any Turkish territory. In addition, Armenia is required to respect Turkey's territorial integrity by virtue of commitments made by states participating in the Organization for Security and Cooperation in Europe. Armenia is further bound by the 1921 Treaty of Moscow and the Treaty of Kars, which demarcated the boundary between Turkey and Armenia. Article 17 of the Kars treaty provides that there will be "uninterrupted communication between the two countries" and obligates both to take "the necessary measures for the maintenance and development of railway, telegraph and other means of communication, as well as to secure the free movement of persons and goods." In accordance with the Vienna Convention on the Law of Treaties and the Convention on Succession of States, the Republic of Turkey and the Republic of Armenia have chosen to inherit these treaty obligations.[4]

In addition to its practical benefits, Gul was reminded that opening the border would enhance worldwide esteem for Turkey. The 2004 NATO summit in Turkey would provide an ideal platform for Ankara to profile its role as gateway to the Caucasus, as a moderating influence in the Near East, and as a positive force in Iraq. Gul took these arguments on board and insisted, "We want to restore our relations with Armenia." However, he emphasized that Turkey would not act under duress.[5] Until the congressional resolutions had fully run their course, Ankara would take no action.

Senior administration officials intervened to counter congressional efforts commemorating the fifteenth anniversary of America's signing of the Genocide Convention, which mentioned the Armenian genocide. Cheney worked the phones and was assured by Dennis Hastert that H.R.

193 would be kept from the House floor. Similarly Senate majority leader Bill Frist (R-TN) and Dick Lugar (R-IN), chairman of the Senate Foreign Relations Committee, promised to suppress S.R. 307.

At the end of July, Congress recessed until Labor Day. I hoped that Ankara would quietly open its border sometime during the dead of summer, when everyone was on holiday and not paying attention. To assure Ankara, Vartan Oskanian reiterated that Armenia was prepared to normalize relations with Turkey without preconditions, such as recognition of the Armenian genocide.

At a critical point in Ankara's deliberations, the Dashnak Party launched a nonsensical campaign to keep the border closed. Vahan Hovhannessian, ARF's vice chairman, indicated that "Re-opening of the Armenian-Turkish border is a danger to Armenia's national interests. It is my deep conviction that opening the Armenian–Turkish border puts the interests of Armenia under direct threat." He continued, "Armenia is not yet ready to open the border. The country would be flooded by cheap goods from Turkey and Armenia's farmers would be especially hard hit."[6] Though Dashnaks are the junior partner in Kocharian's governing coalition, they have remarkable sway over the Armenian president. In contradiction to the Armenian government's official position, the Dashnaks insist that Turkey return territory and pay compensation before Armenia will agree to open its border. The Dashnaks are similar to rejectionists in Turkey, who justify their existence by opposing progress. In a further demonstration of pettiness, the Dashnaks also ridiculed the proposal to establish a Turkish-Armenian parliamentary "Friendship Group." Hovhannessian claimed that Turkish-Armenian cooperation would lead to an "absurd situation."[7]

If Ankara was in fact on the verge of opening its border, its decision was delayed by the illness of Haider Aliev. He collapsed during a public address and was rushed from Baku to a hospital in Ankara. Before being moved to the world-famous Cleveland clinic coronary unit, Aliev named his son to the post of prime minister. Hopes that Ilham Aliev would be more conciliatory were soon dashed. He called on all Azeri nongovernmental organizations to halt contacts with their Armenian counterparts until the dispute over Nagorno-Karabakh was resolved. "Do not enter into any relations with the aggressor state," warned Ilham.[8]

In August, Ilter Turkmen and I met at a seaside restaurant in Bodrum. He was pessimistic about the border opening. Azerbaijan's strong lobby in Turkey would protest. Wise in the ways of Turkey's establishment, Ilter felt that no decision would be forthcoming prior to Azerbaijan's presidential elections in October. Ankara would never act with Haider Aliev on his deathbed. Such a decision would insult his legacy.

The grave difficulties in postwar Iraq also affected Ankara's decision. As security conditions worsened in Iraq, Ankara became convinced that the Bush administration would come running for help. General Abizaid, commander in chief of the U.S. Central Command, and European Commander General James Jones went to Ankara to discuss security cooperation in Iraq. Their visit in July 2003 was immediately followed by a series of bombings and assassinations. A car bomb was used to attack the Jordanian embassy in Baghdad. Days later, Sergio Vieira de Mello and twenty-one UN colleagues perished when the UN compound was also attacked. Soon after, the popular Arab Shiite leader, Bakr al-Hakim, and Akila Hashemi, a member of the newly appointed Iraqi Governing Council, were murdered. The spiral of violence was getting out of control.

The Washington Institute's Soner Cagaptay indicated that "Turkey has a major role to play in the reconstruction of Iraq, both in terms of short-term economic reconstruction but also in terms of the wider, ideological aspects of reconstruction."[9] The Coalition Provisional Authority took steps to expand Turkey's role in the fields of humanitarian and reconstruction assistance. A delegation from the Kirkuk chamber of commerce visited Istanbul to explore trade and investment opportunities. In a nod to Turkey's concern about PKK guerillas in the mountains of northern Iraq, U.S. military planners agreed to demilitarize the group, which is on the U.S. list of terrorist organizations. The Bush administration put priority on internationalizing the security presence in Iraq. When India, Pakistan, and South Korea bowed out, Turkey became the most likely country to deploy troops.

On October 7, the Turkish parliament voted 358 to 183 authorizing the deployment of troops to Iraq. The Turkish embassy in Washington, D.C., announced that:

> The decision is a major demonstration by Turkey of its friendship, longstanding alliance and partnership with the U.S. and the American people. Turkey's move towards contributing to peace and stability in Iraq is very significant in light of the war against terrorism. Having participated in Operation Enduring Freedom and then assumed command of the International Security Assistance Force (ISAF) in Afghanistan, the deployment of Turkish peacekeeping troops in Iraq will essentially uphold a tradition dating back to the Korean War of Turkish and U.S. troops serving side by side to promote shared goals and uphold common values.[10]

With the Bush administration preoccupied by Iraq, U.S. pressure on Ankara to open the Turkish-Armenian border all but disappeared. By the time Gul and Oskanian met in New York on September 23, Gul knew he had the upper hand. In a bland statement, Armenia's Ministry of Foreign Affairs indicated that "They discussed bilateral concerns, including prospects for opening the border between the two countries. They agreed to meet again and to continue to talk about the steps necessary toward normalization of relations."[11]

* * *

Lacking U.S. pressure and with bilateral talks between Turkey and Armenia seemingly at a stalemate, I convened a meeting of mayors from small cities in the bordering provinces of Armenia, Azerbaijan, Georgia, and Turkey. The group had been meeting regularly to explore trade opportunities and avenues for contact and cooperation. I encouraged them to mobilize key constituencies calling for an opening of the border.

We met at Vera Palace Hotel in Tbilisi, a depressing old structure tucked away in a run-down part of Georgia's capital. Our dinner table was crowded with cold meats and mayonnaise salads. We dined by candlelight. The electricity was intermittent and we were plunged into darkness several times. The flickering lights were emblematic of their expectations. Though everyone looked forward to a brighter future, they were all too familiar with everyday constraints to progress.

The Armenians came armed with a portfolio of projects, ranging from trade to tourism, as well as cultural and civic exchanges. Though Azeris are keen to cooperate, they face practical limits. They know Aliev's authoritarian tendencies and are careful not to run afoul of the central government. Georgia is the only country in the South Caucasus maintaining good relations with all its neighbors.

Turks are more pragmatic and, therefore, wary of commitments. When the Turkish mayor of Kars took the initiative to invite the Armenian mayor of Gyumri for a visit in 2001, he was hauled before the state security court and charged with crimes against the state. At the Tbilisi meeting, Turkish representatives expressed support for opening the border and normalizing regional trade relations. When the group proposed a joint statement, the Turks wavered. They know all too well that disagreeing with Ankara could put them in jail.

The mayors agreed to focus on small steps allowable in the current climate. They also agreed on measures capitalizing on new opportunities in the event that the Turkish-Armenian border was opened. Though Ankara granted permission for "Flyair" to commence direct flights between Istanbul and Yerevan on October 16, 2003, the decision fell far short of opening the border to normal travel and trade. To break the logjam, U.S. officials proposed that the border be opened for diplomatic passport holders or third-country nationals. As of this writing, no action has been taken.

My heart ached as the mayors stood on the steps of the Vera Hotel waving goodbye. No matter their effort, they are profoundly constrained by the limitations imposed by their governments. Despite their apparent optimism, they seemed to know that the world had moved on and left them behind.

* * *

On April 14, 2004, TARC agreed that its work as a commission was ending. TARC's term was to be one year, but the course of events required it to exist longer than intended.

Partly as a result of its efforts, TARC believes civil society contracts are now permanent and that official contacts will also continue. A new and larger Turkish-Armenian Consultative Group has been established to meet annually, review progress, and make recommendations. In his 2004 Remembrance Day statement, President Bush indicated: "On this day I commend individuals in Armenia and Turkey who have worked to support peace and reconciliation, including through the Turkish-Armenian Reconciliation Commission."[12]

Tevan Poghosyan believes there is a difference between physical and psychological borders. He explained that Turks and Armenians shared a deep distrust and animosity toward one another when the Track Two program was first launched. Tevan insisted they have made great progress. "Today peoples of the two nations are talking about relations more freely and with fewer prejudices." Ever hopeful, he assured me, "Even though the physical border remains, the psychological barrier has been broken."[13]

Notes

1. Rosbalt, July 14, 2003.
2. Schleifer, "U.S. seeks Turkish troops," July 22, 2003.
3. Statement by Colin Powell, July 24, 2003.
4. Soviet Documents on Foreign Policy, October 1921.
5. Rosbalt, July 14, 2003.
6. *ARMINFO,* July 14, 2003.
7. Ibid.
8. "Azeri PM Calls for an End to Civic Contacts with 'Aggressor' Armenia," *Armenia Liberty,* September 11, 2003.
9. Schleifer, "U.S. seeks Turkish troops."
10. Statement issued by the Turkish embassy in Washington, D.C., October 8, 2003.
11. Press release issued by the Armenian Ministry of Foreign Affairs, September 25, 2003.
12. The White House, April 24, 2004.
13. Meeting notes, September 25, 2003.

14

FROM THEORY TO PRACTICE

The world is full of conflicts that could benefit from Track Two. To enhance prospects for peaceful resolution of conflicts, other efforts should consider lessons learned from the *Track Two Program on Turkey and the Caucasus*.

The following definitions, concerns and strategies can be used by practitioners during the development and implementation of a Track Two endeavor.

Track One

Official diplomacy is conducted by authorized representatives of the United States government. Foreign Service Officers (FSOs) all too often limit themselves to delivering formal messages as instructed by the State Department. They also gather information and impressions to inform the making of American foreign policy.

Instead of reaching out to average citizens in countries where they work, diplomats frequently rely on contact with other diplomats and the country's elite. FSOs often are inhibited about interacting outside of official channels. They require authorization just to meet outside the embassy. Limited contact with nonstate actors often leads to official policy based on incomplete information, slanted perceptions, or inaccurate assessments.

The State Department includes many quality individuals with vast knowledge of the world. However, the Department inculcates a risk-averse culture that discourages initiative and stifles creativity. In discussions with foreign nationals, they are reluctant to try out new ideas lest they be misinterpreted as official government policy. As protectors of U.S. interests, American diplomats are trained to bargain from established positions.

U.S. officials employ a combination of cooperative and competitive negotiating strategies. In a cooperative mode, diplomats emphasize positive self-interest as well as mutual benefit. This allows them to focus on similar beliefs and shared interests. Their demeanor is open to communication, ready to listen, respond, and be helpful. The negotiator enhances mutual power rather than power differences.

A cooperative mode, however, is not the only course. The struggle for power is a distinguishing mark of politics among nations. When interests collide, U.S. diplomats may abandon collaboration and pursue a more adversarial approach. The cooperative negotiating model gives way to a competitive one when negotiations break down and feelings of suspicion and hostility prevail.

Track Two

Informal third-party mediation is not new. Nor is the notion of finding some way of getting conflicting groups together to discuss their differences. Undertaken in consultation with government officials, Track Two adds value to official diplomacy. Track Two is not a substitute for official diplomatic efforts. However, its flexibility helps compensate for the inherent constraints on officials.

As an unofficial exercise in problem solving, Track Two has evolved over decades of engagement by private citizens in developing ideas and experimenting with solutions. Nonstate actors are able to creatively explore the underlying conditions that give rise to conflict and develop joint strategies for addressing shared problems through reciprocal efforts. The goal is to foster collaboration so that conflict comes to be seen as a shared problem requiring the cooperation of both sides.[1]

A critical mass of individuals who perceive an alternative to violence can trigger diplomatic activity or consolidate the progress of existing diplomatic efforts. Support for peace demonstrates to political leaders that their polity is prepared for change even if they are not. Even when official diplomatic channels are working, Track Two can enhance the efforts of government representatives. Should official diplomacy fail, Track Two also serves as a safety net. Track Two is more effective when it involves a democratic government that is open to the ideas and initiatives of its polity.

Cycle of Violence

Conflict often involves a cycle of deadly violence. Many conflicts are rooted in the need for recognition, particularly when group trauma has occurred. Historic loss shapes identity formation, which in turn binds members of a clan together through their shared suffering. Issues of identity, trauma, and fear typically constitute the basis of conflict.

Reflecting on the psychology of victimization, Joe Montville points out that "Human beings experience varying levels of anxiety about their safety and survival. By adhering to the institutions of family, work and society, human beings develop tangible and psychological defenses against unexpected negative events." When threatened, individuals may resort to traditional human defensive thinking, including the use of violence. Even the aggressor tends to adopt feelings of victimization to justify wrongs they may have committed. When the suffering of one party is recognized, both the victim and the victimizer have a greater ability to recognize the needs of others.[2]

Vamik Volkan has pioneered psychological work exploring the underlying attitudes giving rise to conflict. He focuses on the psychodrama of conflict to help humanize the adversary relationship, recognize grievances, and ultimately catalyze forgiveness. Vamik maintains that recognizing historic wounds is the first step in conflict resolution. The next step is accepting responsibility and mourning losses. Cultivating empathy can lead to an apology, which, in turn, enables progress and healing. He believes that the process of mutual acknowledgment is fundamental to breaking the cycle of accusation, recrimination, and violence.[3]

Ripeness

Track Two emphasizes creating conditions of ripeness so that parties to a conflict can move from confrontation to communication and then to cooperation. The dynamics of conflict are not static. Progress can be accelerated by measures that are intended to reduce tension. Solutions are not possible unless the problem is ripe for resolution.

In his address to the Knesset in November 1977, Egypt's president Anwar el-Sadat heralded progress but noted, "There remains another wall. This wall constitutes a psychological barrier between us, a barrier of suspicion, a barrier of rejection; a barrier of fear, of deception."[4] Sixteen years later, the situation had changed. After meeting King Hussein of Jordan in July 1994, President Yitzhak Rabin felt there had been a breakthrough and that a psychological barrier had been passed.[5]

Parties to a conflict are ready to negotiate when they believe it is in their interest, when they tire of violence, or when they become sufficiently frustrated with the status quo. Disputants must come to a point where they recognize that the present stalemate does not advance their real interests. Before engaging with the adversary, it is important to recognize that a solution can be achieved and to believe that a mutually acceptable agreement is possible.

Ripeness arises when there is a strong motivation to reach an agreement influenced by contextual factors as well as the individual's subjective attitude toward the conflict. Even if parties to a dispute are willing to begin a dialogue, they must overcome behavioral obstacles. Well-established patterns of hostility and miscommunication are usually exacerbated by a lack of problem-solving skills.

The Role of Facilitation

An experienced Track Two facilitator is indispensable. To develop an orderly mediation process, the facilitator must overcome skepticism and earn the respect of both sides. Active listening allows the facilitator to distinguish between needs and positions. It also enables the facilitator to encourage an appreciation for other perspectives and to reframe issues emphasizing common ground. By effectively guiding the dialogue process, the facilitator can increase the motivation of parties to take steps toward an agreement.

To inspire confidence, the facilitator must demonstrate a substantive knowledge of the issues. The facilitator must also develop a good working relationship by fostering open communication, being responsive to suggestions, and seeking feedback. Trust is realized when the facilitator is perceived as balanced and neutral. The facilitator inspires confidence by highlighting possibilities and assuring parties they can act without losing face. Responsibility for establishing a cooperative problem-solving environment rests with the facilitator. When confusion arises, he/she must provide clarity. When options narrow, he/she must expand the range of possibilities. When ideas are put forward, he/she must assist in a realistic assessment of their viability.

It is important to beware of amateurism. Landrum Bolling warns that "When private individuals set out actively to mediate or to search for solutions to tough international problems, they must know what they are doing."[6] In some cases, there may only be one chance to initiate a Track Two process.

Project Development

Track Two is a flexible mechanism that adjusts to adversity and responds to opportunity. The stages of Track Two project development are contact, communication, and cooperation. Since conflicts are not the same, there is no standard approach. To justify the effort and cost, Track Two must be proactive, entrepreneurial, and results-oriented.

Developing a Track Two project starts with a thorough analysis of the needs, values, and interests of parties to the dispute. The facilitator should have expertise in project development, as well as knowledge of the culture and other relevant conditions. Understanding the nuances of a conflict requires extensive study, as well as personal interaction. In addition to scholarly research, it is important to visit the target countries in order to establish contact with parties on all sides of the conflict. It is also useful to interview government officials steeped in the issue. In addition to the U.S. ambassador, interviews should be conducted with various sections of an embassy, including political, economic, and public affairs officers. Meeting officials from other concerned governments is essential. The delegation of the European Commission conducts insightful analysis. Norway and other countries with generous development assistance budgets offer a fresh perspective.

Research should also assess the role of international stakeholders—multilateral organizations, governments, businesses, and NGOs—who influence the behavior of key national and local actors. Evaluating stakeholders helps to determine other mediation efforts that are under way. It is important to avoid a multiplicity of efforts and to make sure that the Track Two endeavor does not detract from other initiatives.

Structure

The following Track Two mechanisms can be undertaken individually or in combination:

- *Back-Channels* are officially authorized for passing messages or conducting negotiations when formal methods of communication are ineffective. However, Track Two is not typically a secret process aimed at supplanting the efforts of official diplomacy. Diplomats hate surprises and are distrustful of unofficial intermediaries engaged without their knowledge.
- *The Policy Forum* sets the stage for official discussions by developing new ideas that inform formal negotiations. Negotiators always feel an urgent need for progress and rarely have the opportunity to step back and develop a vision for future relations that meets the needs of both sides. The policy forum assumes a visionary function by looking ahead at issues not yet on the official agenda and defining alternatives tested in discussion. It can serve as either the prelude or a backup to official negotiations. It also acts as a safety net. If an incident causes a rupture

in diplomatic relations, the policy forum can help open dialogue or be transformed into a back-channel.

- *The Media Group* focuses on images of "the other" to reduce negative stereotypes justifying violence. For rapprochement to occur, it is necessary to create a public opinion environment conducive to conflict resolution. Conflict resolution media includes jointly produced news, documentary, and children's television. Conflict resolution radio is produced in news, drama, and call-in formats. Print media employs joint features, coauthored editorials, shared reference services, staff exchanges, and information hotlines. It is also used to shape public opinion, making it safer for political leaders to take risks and enhancing transparency holding governments accountable.

- *Technical Cooperation* develops shared interests between professionals and emphasizes tangible benefits. Collaboration builds bonds, blurs national boundaries, and reduces hostile images. Track Two involving business leaders often results in proposals for cooperative economic development. By focusing on the economic effect of conflict, business leaders are often able to envision the practical benefits to collaboration. They are a key constituency with the ability to influence political leaders.

- *The Psychology Workshop* explores issues of identity, trauma, and fear constituting the basis for conflict. Conflict is often rooted in the need for recognition, particularly when group trauma has occurred. The psychology workshop offers a facilitated environment to humanize the adversary relationship, recognize grievances, and mourn losses. Cultivating empathy breaks the cycle of accusation, recrimination, and violence. It can lead to an apology, which, in turn, enables progress and healing. The results of the psychology workshop should be disseminated via the media to humanize the adversarial relationship, influence public opinion, and inform activities of the policy forum.

Other types of Track Two activities include grassroots networks and people-to-people contact.

Participants

Group chemistry is important. Personal bonds can be achieved not only in structured discussions, but also by sharing meals, cultural events, and recreational activities. Adversaries come to know one another by interacting. In knowing, they can favorably alter negative images and find alternatives to the use of violence for settling disputes. At first, participants usually meet at a neutral site or in a third country to build confidence, identify practical steps, and explore mutually satisfactory outcomes.

The facilitator should develop criteria for participants and counter political pressures by retaining ultimate authority for their selection. When seeking to influence policy, participants should be politically well connected and have access to their government or political parties. Governments change; therefore, participants should be drawn from across the political spectrum. Private citizens have greater latitude to critique existing policies and help educate officials on the realities of a situation.

Participants are busy people with competing demands on their time. They must feel that their effort could amount to something. Participants with whom the facilitator has a personal or institutional relationship are preferable. Though a Track Two process may include vested interests opposed to a solution, participants must be genuinely committed to rapprochement. Ill-intended individuals can upset the group dynamic and set back the goal of reconciliation. Some persons seem to always attend international meetings. While Track Two experience is desirable, efforts should be made to avoid the "same old faces."

The Facilitator

A robust facilitator helps participants envision new possibilities for cooperation. In consultation with participants, the facilitator assesses the degree of ripeness for resolving the conflict. The facilitator inspires confidence by working toward realizable goals and demonstrating attributes worthy of trust and respect. It is important to establish credibility early in the process by working closely with participants and demonstrating concrete results.

The facilitator should have language skills and interpersonal and facilitation expertise. The facilitator will not have all the answers. He/she may be joined by a professional with suitable technical credentials. The expert becomes a resource person who actively participates in discussions and, as necessary, conducts team-building workshops and training sessions.

Ground Rules

Strong leadership is especially important during the sensitive first phases of a project when goals are being determined, agendas set, and procedures finalized. While making participants feel as though they have ownership of the process, the facilitator must not surrender control or decision-making authority.

Procedures should be discussed and agreed to by the group. Participants must adhere to basic protocols, such as showing respect and allowing others to speak without interruption. Working together as a group to set goals and plan strategies helps develop a sense of common purpose. Previous or comparable efforts should be assessed in order to avoid duplication.

The physical environment affects the attitude of participants. Initial meetings should be convened on neutral ground and in comfortable settings. The meetings should be long enough so they are substantive, but not so long that they allow participants to focus on areas of disagreement. There will be times when anger surfaces and hostility prevails. Participants must be allowed to express their feelings. While allowing free expression, the facilitator must keep the conversation from becoming too acrimonious. In addition to structured discussions, the agenda should include lots of coffee breaks so that meeting participants can interact on the margins of formal discussions. When participants are bogged down by their narrow preconceptions, inviting luminaries can help inspire and motivate.

Communications Strategy

The facilitator must establish ground rules governing confidentiality and record keeping. It is useful to chronicle discussions so that agreements are highlighted and commitments codified. However, minutes of the meeting should be avoided, as they inhibit free discussion. Though preparing a text or joint statement is advisable, it can become a distraction or a subject of disagreement. While sometimes negotiating a joint text can help focus discussions, a chairman's statement is usually the most efficient way of keeping records, clarifying commitments, and highlighting common ground.

Information should be disseminated strategically to advance project objectives at different stages of project development. Media guidelines help avoid misrepresentation and misunderstandings. Participants should:

- Issue an initial statement of purpose addressing questions about mandate and legitimacy.
- Keep in confidence activities and discussions, unless otherwise agreed.
- Represent views in an individual capacity, not on behalf of the group as a whole.
- Seek consent from both sides prior to attributing remarks to the group, and, prior to attributing remarks to any individual, seek consent from that individual.
- Speak or write constructively about the group's efforts and its members.

- Speak or write without constraint in capacities other than as a member of the group.
- Represent accurately any and all matters.
- Call to the attention of the facilitator statements or writing that are inconsistent with agreed media principles so that the facilitator can relay concerns to the group.

Government Relations

The overarching goal of Track Two is to shape policy and influence events. To this end, Track Two targets policy-makers and opinion leaders. Like official diplomacy, Track Two is affected by the official climate. When official relations are warmer, counterparts are encouraged by their authorities to explore issues more creatively. Similarly, a chill over official relations constrains participants in a Track Two process.

Contact with governments is a tricky business. On the one hand, contact with U.S. and other government officials enhances credibility by creating the perception of influence. On the other, it is important to assert independence from governments in order to preserve impartiality. To establish a portal into the policy-making process, the coordinator should stay in touch with government officials. Establishing a working-level point of contact ensures that the official bureaucracy will pay attention.

Though it is important to stay in touch with official actors, Track Two must maintain its independence from governments. When it is perceived that participants are acting on behalf of their government, their contribution is resented. A dialogue that merely repeats what is going on in official negotiations is unsustainable in a Track Two format. Participants should be independent from their governments. Even the participation of individuals who are government consultants can raise questions about the initiative's independence and integrity.

"Track one and a half" is when government officials meet in their private capacity at a forum convened by a neutral NGO. The term also applies to meetings between parliamentarians who, as politicians, are neither duly appointed representatives of their government nor merely civil society representatives. Track one and a half may be used when the political will is lacking or as a transition from Track Two to official diplomacy.

Financing

Fund-raising is always an issue. While the financial support of governments and private grant-makers is welcome, it does not entitle them to control. Manipulation by officials leads to charges that Track Two is a waste of time or that the governments themselves should be getting on with the job. Detractors may accuse the official sponsor of using Track Two as a way to avoid direct negotiations or as a substitute for politically difficult decisions.

Track Two will flounder if its integrity is compromised by either participants or the organizer. Funds must not be accepted from any sponsor with a direct interest in the outcome. To avoid the appearance of political manipulation, funding should be secured from diversified sources. Potential funders include concerned governments as well as private grant-makers.

Funding decisions are usually made in the field. Some embassies have discretionary funds for small grants. Even when decisions about larger grants are made at headquarters, government officials always seek input from the embassy or field personnel. The same is true for private grant-makers who typically have decentralized decision-making.

Track Two participants must feel that the sponsoring organization has adequate resources to make a serious commitment. If the initial brainstorming session goes well, resources must be available to build on momentum by quickly convening a follow-up meeting. Initial fund-raising should anticipate the costs of several meetings.

Staffing

Effective project management is best served by a team of professionals with complementary expertise. The project director should be politically savvy and well connected. He/she must be able to syncopate activities with official diplomacy and have experience in project design, development, and evaluation. In addition to headquarters operations, regular visits to the field or maintaining a presence on the ground helps troubleshooting and enhances project management.

Interdisciplinary staff is needed to manage complex international projects. The project director provides overall strategic direction and liaises with policy-makers and funders. The facilitator designs the working group meetings and manages the dialogue process. The resource person is a technical specialist who supports working groups with information and training. The secretariat organizes logistics, manages administration, maintains project databases, disseminates materials, sustains communications, and coordinates travel. The secretariat also conducts research and maintains a database of civil society contacts and cooperative projects. The database measures progress and documents the emergence of a conflict resolution Track Two community.

The *Track Two Program on Turkey and the Caucasus* can be used to inform comparable future endeavors. Premature publicity is the enemy of progress. Discretion is essential during the initial phase; so is a careful management of media relations thereafter. Events outside of one's control will inevitably disrupt the process. It is necessary to be flexible in adapting strategies to external events. Track Two is not worth the time or money unless it achieves something. While activities should be coordinated with concerned governments, measures are needed to avoid official manipulation.

Track Two rarely results in a breakthrough. As evidenced by TARC, reconciliation is a painful and difficult process full of pitfalls. It is like riding a bicycle. You fall off when you stop pedaling.

Notes

1. Herbert C. Kelman, "The Problem-Solving Workshop in Conflict Resolution," in *Unofficial Diplomats,* edited by Maureen R. Berman and Joseph E. Johnson, Columbia University Press, 1977.
2. Joseph V. Montville, "Transnationalism and the Role of Track Two Diplomacy," in *Approaches to Peace: An Intellectual Map,* edited by W. Scott Thompson and Kenneth M. Jensen, U.S. Institute for Peace Press, 1991.
3. Vamik Volkan, "The Need to Have Enemies and Allies: A Development Approach," *Political Psychology,* June 1985.
4. President el-Sadat, The Knesset, Jerusalem, November 20,1977.
5. "The Washington Declaration," July 25, 1994, and White House Press Release, Office of the Press Secretary, July 25, 1994.
6. Landrum Bolling, "Strengths and Weaknesses of Track Two: A Personal Account," *Conflict Resolution: Track Two Diplomacy,* edited by Diane B. Bendahmane and John W. McDonald, Center for the Study of Foreign Affairs, Foreign Service Institute, Government Printing Office, 1987.

EPILOGUE

We were delayed in traffic on one of Istanbul's busy thoroughfares. I was accompanying some Armenians back to their hotel when one turned to me and asked, "You believe there was genocide, don't you?"

His question took me by surprise. As a humanitarian activist, I have a natural affinity for the underdog. I strongly oppose moral equivalency that blurs distinctions between the victim and the aggressor, and between right and wrong. I awkwardly explained that I could not possibly serve as an objective facilitator if I was partial to one side or the other. My only interest was enabling Turks and Armenians to discuss their differences, acknowledge the past, and move on. My job was limited to creating a context for politically influential people to develop new understandings, insights, and ideas.

I was impressed by the character and courage of many participants in the *Track Two Program on Turkey and the Caucasus*. They worked hard to advance the goal of reconciliation. Many rose to the challenge with grace and dignity. Others were less reliable, at times obstructionist and even mean-spirited.

The September 11 terror attacks and the Iraq war dramatically affected the context of our efforts. In addition, activities were fraught with technical problems. Planes were cancelled; visas were delayed; illness intervened. Turks and Armenians tried to secure my endorsement of their position. Both viewed me with suspicion for not supporting their side.

TARC did not do well managing relations with the media. Members created problems by talking to each other through the press. Finger pointing marred meetings and productive efforts were overwhelmed by the need for damage control. Though TARC endorsed media principles to avoid misrepresentation and misunderstandings, they were adopted too late to

prevent problems. Some TARC members simply ignored them. Short of
expulsion, there was no effective enforcement mechanism.

Soul searching is difficult and painful. I despaired on numerous occasions. When I wanted to withdraw, colleagues stiffened my resolve.
They reminded me that it is important to persevere and to keep going
no matter what. In the end, I feel as though I learned a lot about myself,
and I gained at least as much as I gave to the process.

Despite my optimism, it is important to be realistic about the usefulness of Track Two. I always maintained that Track Two is not a substitute
for official diplomacy. However, Track Two relies on contact with officials
to influence policy. The Track Two program had unparalleled access to
senior officials. It also suffered when the U.S. government neglected our
efforts because its priorities lay elsewhere. Honest self-criticism leads me
to believe that we relied too much on U.S. officials to support our efforts.

* * *

Taking into account these limitations, no one could have predicted
that the process would go so far and so fast. Accomplishments are worth
noting. When TARC was launched, there were no diplomatic contacts
between Turkish and Armenian officials. The border was closed and
visas to Turkey were difficult to obtain. Both peoples felt the heavy burden of history. Relations were defined by distrust.

Through its efforts, TARC:

- Established a structured dialogue and opened the doors for civil soci-
ety contacts between Turks and Armenians.
- Catalyzed diplomatic contact between Turkish and Armenian officials.
- Laid the foundation, through its work with the International Center
for Transitional Justice (ICTJ), for addressing the genocide issue.
- Brought a principled, treaty-based approach to opening the border.

Despite progress, relations between Turkey and Armenia and between
Azerbaijan and Armenia remain volatile. Misunderstandings could easily reverse progress or catalyze a chain of events resulting in violence.

* * *

This book tells TARC's story. I hope that it also serves as a tool for continued discourse between Turks and Armenians. Track Two is a process,
not an event. TARC opened the floodgates and, as a result, thousands of
Turks and Armenians are now able to work together to mutual advantage.

When Marc Grossman hired me as a consultant in 1999, he hoped to
mainstream Track Two as an accepted tool of official diplomacy. On September 23, 2002, he addressed an overflowing conference of NGO rep-

resentatives attending the Secretary's Forum on Track Two Diplomacy. He said, "I believe [Track Two] will be an ever increasing part of our diplomacy. We at the State Department want to be always—always—open to new things—and open to partnerships. Over the years, I've had the chance to practice [Track Two] guided by David Phillips. I worked Track Two in Turkey first between Turks and Kurds, between Turks and Greeks then between Turks and Armenians. The possibilities for Track Two as part and parcel of our diplomacy seem endless."[1] Grossman's acknowledgment was a great honor; I am profoundly grateful for the opportunity to have helped build acceptance of Track Two in the U.S. government.

The Turkish-Armenian border will someday open and normal relations will be established. TARC encountered many obstacles, but its members were able to persevere. Despite difficulties, the satisfaction from being a part of a dynamic process far exceeds its inherent frustrations.

Note

1. Remarks by Undersecretary of State for Political Affairs Marc Grossman at the Secretary's Forum, September 23, 2002.

Turkish Armenian Reconciliation Commission

Recommendations to Concerned Governments
regarding
Improvement of Turkish-Armenian Relations
April 14, 2004

Introduction

The Turkish Armenian Reconciliation Commission (TARC) was formed in Geneva in July 2001 with the express purpose of working to improve relations between Turkey and Armenia and between Turks and Armenians. The primary mechanism for achieving these goals was and is to promote increased contact on both governmental and non-governmental levels. Significant advances have been registered since 2001. These advances have been more visible in the field of civil society, where the most difficult barriers to direct contact are no longer present and the reconciliation process is not only underway but has assumed courses independent of TARC and official relations. Fundamental differences still exist, but the growing movement to engage directly in an effort to resolve them is exactly what TARC was designed to achieve.

Official contacts between the governments have also grown since 2001, but, it must be acknowledged, have not kept pace. Another of TARC's purposes was to make recommendations to governments to promote reconciliation, and since its formation, the Commission has actively done so, both in public and in private. With this document, TARC presents its consensus recommendations on how to improve official relations.

These recommendations are being provided after substantial deliberations. Consultations have been held with concerned representatives of society from many different points of view. While acknowledging the seriousness of the differences, the majority and, clearly, mainstream point of view in Armenian and Turkish societies recognizes the need to promote better relations. Thus, our strong recommendation to the government officials is to actively and publicly encourage contacts and confidence building measures between Turkey and Armenia and within their region.

At the same time, TARC is announcing that its work as a commission is ending. TARC's term was to be one year, but the course of events required a longer period to accomplish our goals. We feel that advances in civil society contacts are now permanent and will only grow in time. We also feel that beyond our recommendations, official relations can now best be continued and advanced independent of the TARC structure. Instead, we have decided to convene an initial meeting of a group larger than TARC's working membership to discuss the subject of Turkish Armenian rapprochement and reconciliation. This conference is planned for the fall of 2004. In addition, we intend to support a new Turkish Armenian consultative group which would meet at least annually to exchange views, review progress, and recommend actions to promote improved relations. TARC's website, *www.tarc.info,* will continue to function under the editorship of one Turkish and one Armenian TARC member. Its mandate is the same as TARC's original purposes and the editors are entrusted with fulfilling that mandate as they see fit.

TARC's progress since 2001 could not have been possible without the critical support of many people and institutions. First among these has been our chairman, David L. Phillips. By publicly thanking him, as well as Ted Sorensen, Alex Borraine and the International Center for Transitional Justice, the Henri Dunant Center, the Vienna Diplomatic Academy, and the Royal United Services Institute, we do not mean to minimize the contributions of so many others who have shared their wisdom, efforts and goodwill towards the cause of a better future for the Turkish and Armenian people. We sincerely thank them all. But, in part, we are making this point just prior to listing our recommendations in order to give officials and others some comfort in knowing that taking risks to improve relations uncovers support from unanticipated places and yields benefits which may not be immediately visible.

Recommendations

Turks and Armenians have a shared heritage. The ultimate goal of the Turkish and Armenian governments should be to have full bilateral diplomatic relations with open social, economic, and cultural activity between the two neighboring countries. Toward this goal of good neighborly relations, we offer the following recommendations:

- *Official Contacts Should Be Further Improved.* Official contacts at the Foreign Minister and other levels have improved substantially since 2001. The presence of Armenian diplomatic representation to the BSEC in Istanbul is to be commended. The governments should accelerate their contacts, devise new frameworks for consultation, and consolidate relations by considering additional treaty arrangements. In the transition to full diplomatic relations, the governments should also consider means of providing diplomatic protection for their nationals in their respective countries.
- *Opening of the Turkish Armenian Border Should Be Announced and Implemented in 2004.* Our recommendation is guided by three factors. First, the treaties between the two countries, while recognizing the existing borders, also call for unhampered transportation and trade across these borders. Second, an open border would significantly improve the economic condition of people living on both sides of the border. Third, an open border is consistent with establishing a basis for normalized bilateral relations and with the international system favored by both countries.
- *The Two Governments Should Publicly Support Civil Society Programs Focused on Education, Science, Culture, and Tourism.* Since 2001, some of the most successful civil society exchanges between Armenians and Turks have taken place in these areas. They deserve credit and encouragement. They also show great promise in dealing with problems in a creative and productive manner. Governments should be more supportive of these efforts by supporting and even initiating programs such as guest lectureships and studies by Turkish and Armenian academics and scientists, joint studies by Turkish and Armenian students, summer studies and targeted scholarship programs, and projects which generate mutual understanding and respect.
- *Standing Mechanisms for Cooperation on Humanitarian Disaster Assistance and Health Care Should Be Established.* Both Armenia and Turkey are prone to natural disasters, most notably (but not exclusively) earthquakes. The record of cooperation in emergencies between the two countries can easily be improved to the benefit of all. In addition, both countries have the opportunity to develop substantial goodwill with each other by increasing and publicizing cooperation in health care and medicine.
- *Security and Confidence Building Measures between Turkey and Armenia Should Be Enhanced.* Our meetings have taught that the overwhelming mainstream of both Turkish and Armenian people desire and are best

served by peaceful relations. In both Turkey and Armenia, security, antiterrorism, and related issues are important concerns. Thus, in the process of improving relations, security issues should be directly addressed through international and regional security arrangements and bilateral contacts in a way that will generate public confidence.

• *Religious Understanding Should Be Encouraged.* Among civil society initiatives, there are also opportunities for religious leaders to develop contacts and engage in joint activities as well as activities within their own groups to promote reconciliation between Turks and Armenians. These activities, including the restoration of religious sites, and supporting the rights and functioning of religious foundations, should be encouraged by governments.

• *The Turkish and Armenian People Need to Develop More Confidence That Their Governments are Working to Surmount the Difficulties Related to the Past.* Those who have followed TARC's work know how difficult this issue was for us. The opinion of the International Center for Transitional Justice (ICTJ) upon our referral for "A Legal Analysis on the Applicability of the United Nations Convention on the Prevention and Punishment of the Crime of Genocide to Events which Occurred During the Early Twentieth Century" is on our website for consideration.

Conclusion

We conclude with the same idea with which we began this process. There are substantial differences, but there is a growing good faith trend toward resolving these differences. Specifically, that trend is toward moving beyond the state which existed for decades and is strongly in favor of increased direct contacts as a means to mutual understanding. We recognize that some of our recommendations may appear ambitious in the circumstances. In conclusion, therefore, we reemphasize the need for governments to support those who are ready to work for improved relations. Rapprochement and reconciliation, in our case, will be a process and not an event. The difficulty of that process should not be underestimated.

Acronyms

Agency for International Development (AID)
American University (AU)
Armenian Assembly of America (AAA)
Armenian National Committee of America (ANCA)
Armenian Revolutionary Federation (ARF)
Armenian Secret Army for the Liberation of Armenia (ASALA)
Armenian Sociological Association (ASA)
Assembly of Turkish American Associations (ATAA)
Black Sea Economic Cooperation Council (BSEC)
Cable News Network (CNN)
Caucasus International Consortium for Academic Cooperation (CICAC)
Center for the Research of Societal Problems (TOSAM)
Central Intelligence Agency (CIA)
Coalition Provisional Authority (CPA)
Congressional Research Service (CRS)
Educational and Cultural Affairs (ECA)
European Bank for Reconstruction and Development (EBRD)
European Centre for Common Ground (ECCG)
European Parliament (EP)
European Union (EU)
Foreign Service Officer (FSO)
Forum of Armenian Associations in Europe (FAAE)
Freedom of Information Act (FOIA)
Freedom Support Act (FSA)
Front for Advancement and Progress (FRAPH)
Gross Domestic Product (GDP)
Infantry Division (ID)

International Center for Human Development (ICHD)
International Center for Transitional Justice (ICTJ)
International Court of Justice (ICJ)
International Criminal Court (ICC)
International Criminal Tribunal for Yugoslavia (ICTY)
International Monetary Fund (IMF)
International Peace Research Institute, Oslo (PRIO)
International Rescue Committee (IRC)
International Security Assistance Force (ISAF)
Iraqi Turkmen Front (ITF)
Justice and Development Party (AKP)
Kurdistan Democratic Party (KDP)
Kurdistan Workers' Party (PKK)
Marketing Network of the Caucasus (MANEC)
National Intelligence Organization (MIT)
Newly Independent States (NIS)
nongovernmental organization (NGO)
North Atlantic Treaty Organization (NATO)
Organization of the Islamic Conference (OIC)
Organization for Security and Cooperation in Europe (OSCE)
Parliamentarians for Global Action (PGA)
Patriotic Union of Kurdistan (PUK)
Royal United Services Institute (RUSI)
Search for Common Ground (SCG)
Securing Eastern European Democracies (SEED)
Southeastern Brigade (SEEBRIG)
Southeastern Europe Cooperation Initiative (SECI)
Support for Eastern European Democracies (SEED)
Transport Corridor Europe–Caucasus–Asia (TRACECA)
Truth and Reconciliation Commission (TRC)
Turkish-Armenian Business Development Council (TABDC)
Turkish-Armenian Reconciliation Commission (TARC)
Turkish Economic and Social Studies Foundation (TESEV)
Turkish General Staff (TGS)
Turkish Grand National Assembly (TGNA)
Turkish Republic of Northern Cyprus (TRNC)
Union of Manufacturers and Businessmen in Armenia (UMBA)
United States Geological Service (USGS)
United States Government (USG)
United States Information Agency (USIA)
United States Institute of Peace (USIP)
Virtual Agricultural Wholesale Market (VAWM)
World Trade Organization (WTO)

Personalities

John Abizaid:	Commander-in-chief, U.S. Central Command (2004–present).
Rouben Adalian:	Director, Armenian National Institute.
Gunduz Aktan:	Former Undersecretary General of Foreign Affairs of Turkey and ambassador to the United Nations in Geneva; Director of the Turkish Economic and Social Studies Foundation; Turkey's Permanent Representative in Geneva; Advisor to the Prime Minister for Foreign Affairs; and ambassador of Turkey to Greece.
Madeleine Albright:	Former Permanent Representative of the United States to the United Nations (1993–1996) and U.S. Secretary of State (1997–2001).
Heidar Aliev:	President of Azerbaijan (1969–1982 and 1993–2003).
Leila Alieva:	NGO representative from Azerbaijan.
Kofi Annan:	United Nations Secretary General (1997–present).
Richard Armitage:	Deputy Secretary of State (2001–present).
Alexander Arzoumanian:	Former Armenian ambassador to the United Nations (1992–1993) and Foreign Minister (1996–1998).
Devlet Bahceli:	Chairman, Nationalist Action Party (1997–present); Deputy Prime Minister (1999–2002).

Mehmet Baydar:	Turkish Consul General in Los Angeles (until 1973).
Emin Mahir Balcioglu:	Cultural and art expert.
Massoud Barzani:	President, Kurdistan Democratic Party (1979–present).
Halil Berktay:	Professor of History, Sabanci University.
Mehmet Ali Birand:	Turkish journalist.
Edward Blakely:	Dean, Milano School of Management at the New School University.
Alex Boraine:	Deputy Director, South African Truth and Reconciliation Commission and President of the International Center for Transitional Justice.
Zbigniew Brzezinski:	U.S. National Security Adviser (1977–1981).
Sam Brownback:	Republican Congressman from Kansas (1994–1996); Republican Senator from Kansas (1996–present).
Soner Cagaptay:	Senior Fellow, Washington Institute for Near East Policy.
Ismail Cem:	Foreign Minister of Turkey (1997–present).
Richard Cheney:	U.S. Defense Secretary (1989–1993) and Vice President (2001–present).
Tansu Ciller:	Prime Minister of Turkey (1993–1995).
Glafco Clerides:	Former President, Republic of Cyprus (1993–2003).
John Connor:	Senator from Ireland.
Jon S. Corzine:	Democratic Senator from New Jersey (2000–present).
Stepan Demirchian:	Chairman, People's Party of Armenia; Armenian MP
Rauf Denktash:	Turkish Cypriot leader.
Edward P. Djerejian:	Founding Director of the James A. Baker Institute at Rice University; former Assistant Secretary of State for Near Eastern Affairs; and former U.S. ambassador to Israel and to the Syrian Arab Republic.
Zoran Djindjic:	Prime Minister of Serbia (2001–2003).
Bulent Ecevit:	Prime Minister of Turkey (1974, 1977–1979, 1999–2002).
Abulfez Elcibey:	President of Azerbaijan (1992–1993).
Sukru Elekdag:	Former ambassador of Turkey to the United States (1979–1989).

Jon Ensign:	Republican Congressman from Nevada (1995–1999); Republican Senator from Nevada (2000–present).
Necmettin Erbakan:	Prime Minister of Turkey (1996–1997).
Recep Tayyip Erdogan:	Prime Minister of Turkey (2003–present).
Dogu Ergil:	Member of the Political Science Faculty at Ankara University and Director of the Foundation for the Research of Societal Problems in Turkey.
Ustun Erguder:	Director, Istanbul Policy Center at Sabanci University.
Sadi Erguvenc:	Former General in the Turkish Air Force.
Ahmet Ertegun:	Chairman, Atlantic Records.
Ahmet Evin:	Faculty member, Sabanci University.
Douglas Feith:	U.S. Undersecretary of Defense for Policy (2001–present); former lobbyist for Republic of Turkey .
Helena Kane Finn:	Counselor for Public Affairs, U.S. Embassy Ankara, Turkey (1997–2000); Acting/Assistant Secretary of State for Educational and Cultural Affairs (2001).
Tommy Franks:	Commander-in-chief, U.S. Central Command (2000–2003).
Douglas Frantz:	Former *New York Times* correspondent in Istanbul.
Dan Fried:	Deputy Assistant Secretary of State for the Newly Independent States (2000–2001) and Director for European Affairs at the National Security Council (2001–present).
Bill Frist:	Republican Senator from Tennessee (1994–present).
Harry Gilmore:	U.S. ambassador to the Republic of Armenia (1993–1995).
Marc Grossman:	Undersecretary of State for Political Affairs (2001–2005); Assistant Secretary of State for European and Canadian Affairs (1997–1998); and U.S. ambassador to Turkey (1995–1997).
Abdullah Gul:	Foreign Minister of Turkey (2003–present).
Ken Hachikian:	Chairman, Armenian National Committee of America.
Shelley Hack:	Media consultant.

Richard Hagopian:	Armenian-American performer of traditional Armenian music
Abdul Hamid:	Sultan of the Ottoman Empire (1876–1909).
Lord David Hannay:	United Kingdom Special Negotiator for Cyprus (1996–2003); ambassador and Permanent Representative to the EC (1985–1990); Permanent Representative to the UN (1990–1995); and Independent member of the House of Lords.
J. Dennis Hastert:	Republican Congressman from Illinois (1986–present) and Speaker of the U.S. House of Representatives (1999–present).
Priscilla Hayner:	Director of Outreach and Analysis at the International Center for Transitional Justice.
Richard C. Holbrooke:	U.S. Permanent Representative of the United States to the United Nations (1998–2001); Assistant Secretary of State for European and Canadian Affairs (1994–1995); Assistant Secretary of State for East Asian and Pacific Affairs (1977–1981); and Special Presidential Emissary for Cyprus (1997–1999).
Hrair Hovnannian:	Chairman, Board of Trustees Armenian Assembly of America.
David Hovhanissian:	Former ambassador of Armenia to Syria and Minister-at-large for Regional Issues.
Vahan Hovhannessian:	Vice Chairman, Armenian Revolutionary Federation.
Udi Hrant:	Turkish-Armenian musician.
Hranus Hratyan:	Armenian Women's Group.
General James Jones:	Commander-in-chief, U.S. Forces in Europe.
Jean-Claude Juncker:	Prime Minister of Luxembourg (1995–present).
Robert Kaloosdian:	Chairman, Armenian National Institute; Counselor, Armenian Assembly of America.
Herbert C. Kelman:	Professor, Harvard University.
Mustafa "Ataturk" Kemal:	Founder of modern Turkey and first president of the Republic of Turkey (1923–1938).
Annie Kalayjian:	Professor, Fordham University.
Sule Kilicarslan:	Sociologist and publisher of the Turkish-Armenian Women's Magazine.
Joseph (Joe) Knollenberg:	Republican Congressman from Michigan (1993–present) and co-chairman of the Congressional Caucus on Armenia.

Robert Kocharian: President of the Nagorno Karabakh Republic (1994–1997); Prime Minister of Armenia (1997–1998); and President of Armenia (1998–present).

Sami Kohen: Turkish columnist for *Hurriyet.*

Van Z. Krikorian: New York Attorney; former Armenian Deputy Representative and Counselor to the United Nations (1992); Armenian Assembly of America (1977–present).

Rahmi Koc: Turkish industrialist and former co-chairman of the Greek-Turkish Business Council.

Anthony Lake: U.S. National Security Adviser (1993–1997).

Rafael Lemkin: Author of the Convention on the Prevention and Punishment of the Crime of Genocide.

Michael Lemmon: U.S. ambassador to Armenia (1998–2001).

Richard G. Lugar: Republican Senator from Indiana (1976–present).

Omer Lutem: Former Turkish ambassador to Bulgaria and envoy to the Vatican.

Vazgen Manukian: National Democratic Union, Armenian MP.

Thabo Mbeki: President of South Africa (1999–present).

Justin McCarthy: Professor, University of Louisville.

Mitch McConnell: Republican Senator from Kentucky.

Naira Melkumian: Foreign Minister of Nagorno-Karabakh.

Sergio Vieira de Mello: Special Representative of the Secretary General to Iraq (2003).

Carlos Saul Menem: President of Argentina (1989–1999).

Andranik Markarian: Prime Minister of Armenia (2000–present).

Thomas Miller: Former Cyprus Coordinator and U.S. ambassador to Greece (2002–2004).

Joseph V. Montville: Former U.S. official and "godfather" of Track Two diplomacy.

Henry M. Morgenthau: U.S. ambassador to Turkey (1913–1916).

Mieke Muers: Professor of Economics, American University.

Stephen R. Norton: U.S. Army Colonel (Ret.).

Abdullah Ocalan: Chief of the Kurdistan Worker's Party (PKK).

John Ordway: U.S. ambassador to Armenia (2001–2004).

Vartan Oskanyan: Foreign Minister of Armenia (1998–present).

Turgut Ozal: Prime Minister of Turkey (1983–1989); President of Turkey (1989–1993).

Hilmi Ozkok: Chairman, Turkish General Staff (2002–present).

Frank Pallone:	Democratic Congressman from New Jersey and co-chairman of the Congressional Caucus on Armenia.
Alexis Papahelas:	Greek journalist.
Giorgios Papandreos:	Prime Minister of Greece (1964–1967).
Longin Pastusiak:	President of the Polish Senate (2001–present).
Robert Pearson:	U.S. ambassador to Turkey (2000–2003).
Rachel Pentlarge:	Coordinator of American University's Track Two Program on Turkey and the Caucuses.
Tevan Poghosyan:	Director, International Center for Human Development (Armenia).
Colin Powell:	U.S. Secretary of State (2001–2004); former National Security Advisor; former principal aid to the Secretary of Defense; Four-Star General, served 35 years in the U.S. Army and as Chairman of the Joint Chiefs of Staff.
Samantha Power:	Director, Carr Center for Human Rights at Harvard University and recipient of the Pulitzer Prize (2003).
Kieran Prendergast:	British ambassador to Turkey (1992–1995) and United Nations Undersecretary General for Political Affairs (1997–present).
Yitzhak Rabin:	Prime Minister of Israel (1974–1977, 1992–1995) and recipient of the Nobel Peace Prize (1994).
George Radanovich:	Republican Congressman from California (1994–present).
Shazia Rafi:	Secretary General, Parliamentarians for Global Action.
Champteliers de Ribes:	French prosecutor during the Nurenberg trials.
Condoleeza Rice:	U.S. National Security Adviser (2001–2004).
Jay Rockefeller:	Democratic Senator from West Virginia.
Donald H. Rumsfeld:	Defense Secretary (2001–present).
Sakip Sabanci:	Turkish industrialist (1933–2004).
Anwar el-Sadat:	President of Egypt (1970–1981) and recipient of the Nobel Peace Prize (1978).
William Safire:	Columnist, *The New York Times.*
Ruben Safrastyan:	Professor at Yerevan State University and Director of the Turkish Studies Department at Armenia's National Academy of Sciences, Institute of Oriental Studies.

Abdul Aziz Said:	Professor and the Mohammed Said Farsi Chair of Islamic Peace at American University; and the founding director of the Center for Global Peace, and the International Peace and Conflict Resolution Program at American University.
Ozdem Sanberk:	Former Undersecretary General of Foreign Affairs and Turkey's ambassador to the United Kingdom.
Aram Sarkisian:	Prime Minister of Armenia (1999–2000), leader Republic Party, Armenian MP.
Brent Scowcroft:	U.S. National Security Adviser to Presidents Ford and Bush.
Stephen R. Sestanovich:	Senior Fellow for Russian and Eurasian Studies at the Council on Foreign Relations and former Assistant Secretary of State for the Newly Independent States.
Rouben Shugarian:	Armenian ambassador to America (1992–1999) and Deputy Foreign Minister of Armenia (1999–present).
Orhan Silier:	Director, Turkish History Foundation.
Eduard Simoniants:	Armenia's Former National Security Director (1993–1994).
Calvin Sims:	Editorial Producer, Television Documentary Division, *The New York Times*.
Betty Sitka:	Associate Director, Center for Global Peace at American University.
Theodore C. Sorensen:	Adviser to President John F. Kennedy and board member of the International Center for Transitional Justice.
Kaan Soyak:	Cochairman, Turkish-Armenian Business Development Council.
Noyan Soyak:	Istanbul representative, Turkish-Armenian Business Development Council.
Richard Spring:	Deputy Prime Minister of Ireland (1982–1987, 1993–1994, 1994–1997) and Foreign Minister of Ireland (1993–1994, 1994–1997).
Mumtaz Soysal:	Foreign Minister of Turkey (1994).
Suleiman "the Magnificent":	Sultan of the Ottoman Empire (1520–1566).
Sarik Tara:	President, Enka Holdings (Turkey).
William B. Taylor, Jr:	U.S. ambassador, Afghanistan Coordinator in the U.S. Department of State (2003–present);

	former Coordinator of U.S. Assistance to Europe and Eurasia and Special Deputy Defense Advisor to the U.S. ambassador to NATO.
Levon Ter-Petrossian:	President of Armenia (1991–1998).
George Terzes:	European Center for Common Ground.
Khachig Tololyan:	Professor of English at Wesleyan University, Editor of *Diaspora* Journal.
Ilter Turkmen:	Former Turkish Minister of Foreign Affairs (1980–1983); and former Undersecretary-General of the UN and Commissioner-General of UNRWA.
Desmond Tutu:	Archbishop (1986–1996); Archbishop Emeritus (1996–present); and Director of the South Africa Truth and Reconciliation Commission (1995–2003).
Aghvan Vartanian:	Armenian Revolutionary Federation of Armenia MP.
Vamik Volkan:	Professor of Psychiatry at the University of Virginia.
Elie Wiesel:	Professor of Humanities at Boston University and recipient of the Nobel Peace Prize (1986).
Paul Wolfowitz:	U.S. Deputy Defense Secretary (2001–present).
Tigran Xmalian:	Director, Yerevan Film Studio.
Yasar Yakis:	Foreign Minister of Turkey (2003).
Mehmet Yilmaz:	President, Kars Chamber of Commerce.
Mesut Yilmaz:	Prime Minister of Turkey (1991–1996, 1997–1999).
Paul van Zyl:	Director of Country Programs at the International Center for Transitional Justice and former Executive Secretary for South Africa's Truth and Reconciliation Commission.

NAMES INDEX

You will notice that this
journal contains lined pages
and blank pages. After each
set of six lined pages come
two blank pages. Blank pages
provide opportunities
to sketch, doodle, or write
some more, as you see fit.

My GLACIER NATIONAL PARK Journal

Beginning Date 6/23/21

Ending Date _____

Thank You
for choosing
GLACIER NATIONAL PARK JOURNAL
America's National Parks Series

If you enjoyed the cover art and quality of this product, please give us a thumbs up review on Amazon, Barnes & Noble, iBooks, or other bookseller websites. We sincerely thank you for your patronage and are proud to have provided a vessel for your expression.

www.huzzahpublishing.com

Huzzah Publishing offers several lines of journals in multiple sizes. We are known for our signature cover-art photographs.
If you are interested in purchasing another journal, please check with your retail or online book store.
- Photography Links -
www.miantae.com
www.istock.com and search "miantaemcconnell"
www.shutterstock.com/gallery-4011070p1.html